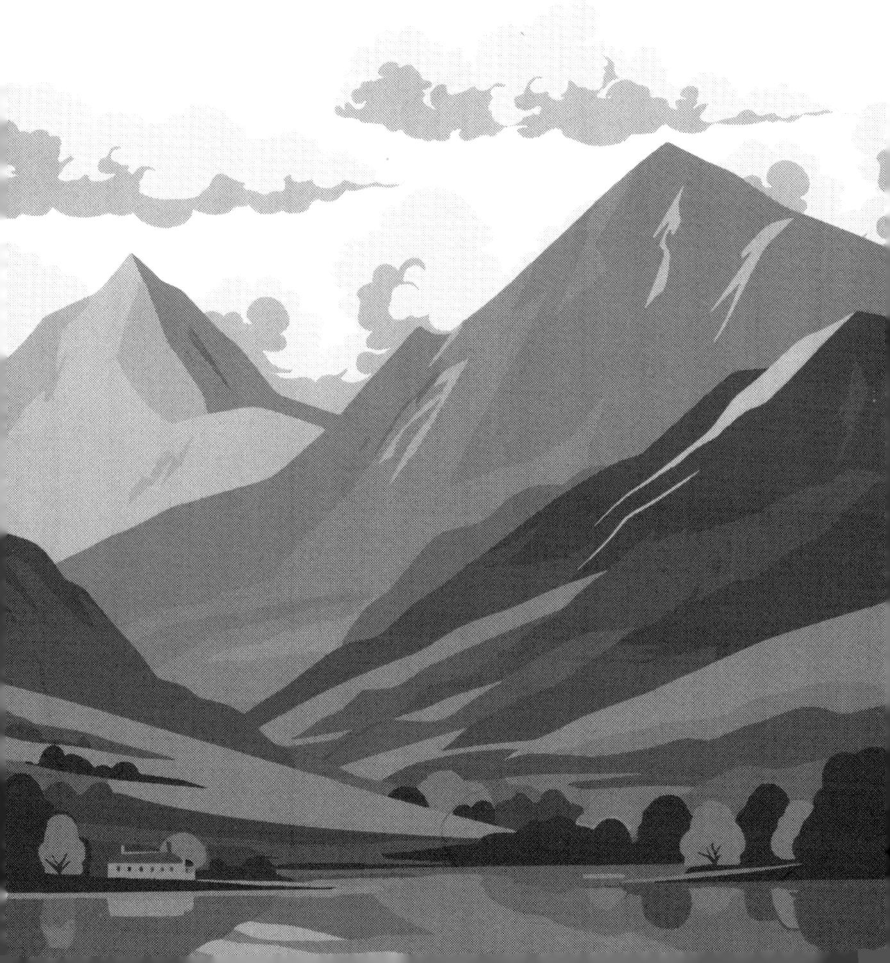

About the Author

Anna Nolan is a Polish linguist, educationalist, author and satirist with a penchant for irreverent satire and comic verse, humour being in her DNA. Besotted with the English language, Anna worked as a teacher of English, broadcaster at the BBC, manager of public examinations and developer of national qualifications in both England and Scotland. Now retired, she writes, climbs Lakeland mountains and leads a walking group.

LAKELAND LARKS, LAUGHTER *and* LUNACIES

ANNA NOLAN

The Book Guild Ltd

First published in Great Britain in 2024 by
The Book Guild Ltd
Unit E2 Airfield Business Park,
Harrison Road, Market Harborough,
Leicestershire. LE16 7UL
Tel: 0116 2792299
www.bookguild.co.uk
Email: info@bookguild.co.uk
X: @bookguild

Copyright © 2024 Anna Nolan

The right of Anna Nolan to be identified as the author of this
work has been asserted by them in accordance with the
Copyright, Design and Patents Act 1988.

All rights reserved. No part of this publication may be
reproduced, transmitted, or stored in a retrieval system, in any form or by any means,
without permission in writing from the publisher, nor be otherwise circulated in
any form of binding or cover other than that in which it is published and without
a similar condition being imposed on the subsequent purchaser.

Typeset in 11pt Minion Pro

Printed on FSC accredited paper
Printed and bound in Great Britain by 4edge Limited

ISBN 978 1916668 942

British Library Cataloguing in Publication Data.
A catalogue record for this book is available from the British Library.

I dedicate this book to my wonderful Skiddaw u3a.

What will enable you to thrive?
And to bedazzle with your drive?
Skiddaw u3a,
Where you'll learn and play,
Make friends, laugh a lot, feel alive!

1

Hilarities and Misunderstandings

People like to know what they are getting for their hard-earned cash, don't they? Too right: we have a cost-of-living crisis on our hands here. I'm sure you wouldn't fancy being like this bloke who thought he was getting a pig:

> There once was this surly big bloke,
> Who purchased a pig in a poke,
> Oh, what a bad deal:
> The pig wouldn't squeal;
> He wasted much dough at a stroke.

So I'll be honest and upfront with you (I hope you will be able to overlook my proclivity for tautology): this exuberant and frolicsome book is shot through with humour, suffused with satire and drenched in comedy, striving to strike a balance between my mountain escapades and mishaps in the English Lake District, jocular musings and satirical asides on anything and everything.

And one of the key sources of hilarity therein is the regrettable fact that I am Polish (some say exceedingly). It's a bummer, but there is nothing I can do about it. You won't believe the extent to which I have tested the lovely British natives because of all the cultural clashes and misunderstandings between us. Take hugs and kisses. A little later, I will introduce you to some of my wonderful friends. As soon as you meet them, you will doubtless appreciate why I would want to lavish affection on them. Until relatively recently, this affection used to manifest itself through effusive hugs and kisses: we Poles are very warm and demonstrative people. So, in Poland, kissing and hugging is commonplace. Naively, I thought that one could do this in Britain. But one can't. Old habits, however, die hard, and I kept on being very Polish. I have to say that my British-born friends seem to have got over their initial shock pretty quickly, withstanding my affectionate eruptions with increasing tolerance. Some even started reciprocating – albeit somewhat limply.

There then came the Big Confession by one of my close friends. She said that, under my Slavonic influence, she had started kissing and hugging her daughters and young grandsons. *What?* She hadn't been kissing and hugging them *already?* So what had she been doing – shaking their hand? Now, it was my turn to be thunderstruck. But there was more. She said that, after she had started behaving in such an uncharacteristically demonstrative manner, her family became seriously concerned that she was saying her goodbyes in anticipation of her imminent expiry! Jeez,

I'd never heard anything as astonishing as this in my entire life. That's a genuine culture clash for you. And it is my bafflement that has spurred me to write this verse.

If you are quite meek,
A peck on the cheek
Will do; it could make someone's day;
However, a kiss,
Full-blown one, is bliss,
Despite what some Britons may say.

A friendly embrace
Is not out of place
In showing affection and care;
Yet some will draw back:
To them, it will smack
Of quite an unseemly affair.

A gentle caress
Is pleasing – unless
One thinks it quite bad for one's style.
I, though, feel so snug
Dispensing a hug,
Enfolding my friends while I smile.

This stiff upper lip
Was surely a blip:
Brits aren't aloof or laconic;
However, some freeze
On feeling my squeeze,
Which is, let's be frank, quite Slavonic.

> I do persevere.
> My friends, I am clear,
> Perceive my warm clasps as worth trying;
> Effusion *this* new
> Does shock – it is true:
> Their kinsfolk lament, "Are you dying?!"

However, all this changed when we were hit by Covid. Obviously, the experience was so horrific for everyone that I have no intention of dwelling on it here. After all, this book is supposed to entertain – not depress – you. But I must mention one pivotal moment, when Vinnie, my lawfully wedded, and I realised, with extraordinary clarity, that things were *really* bad. As always, we turned on the television to watch the latest Covid update. Here is England's chief medical officer, Sir Chris Whitty, whose measured communique is punctuated with, "Next slide, please." We are, of course, used to this by now familiar routine. Then there is Professor Sir Jonathan Van-Tam, the deputy chief medical officer for England, with his usual flourish and knack for analogies. Again, we wouldn't have expected anything less. And then, there is Boris Johnson – *with his hair combed!* Shocked, Vinnie and I look at each other, and it is at that precise instant that we are hit with the awful realisation that the situation must be pretty grim indeed. To this day, I shiver at the memory of this extraordinary vision.

This is when I stopped dispensing my kisses and hugs. Not that it was easy, I can tell you. I have, of course, experienced many more culture clashes on these shores; let me give you another example. When I first heard the phrase 'bucket list', I thought that this was the list of the buckets that the lovely natives were planning to buy. Very much like a shopping list. But, while I fully grasped the rationale behind a shopping list, I couldn't quite fathom why they would draft a list containing one item only. Then – bingo! It *must* have been because of all the consumer choice in a capitalist society. In communist Poland, which I left in the eighties, you would have had only one type of bucket – if you could find a bucket to buy at all, that is. Everything was nationalised, and there was no competition, so why would the government bother producing a range of fancy buckets when it knew full well that it would be able to flog whatever it had knocked up? Obviously, things are very different now: to my delight, Poland is thriving, having been under new management for several decades, but I'm going a long way back here.

Anyway, upon arriving on these welcoming shores, I quickly recognised the enormousness of the gulf between the two worlds. The choice of consumer goods was so bewildering that, when I subsequently encountered the phrase 'choice paralysis', I understood it immediately. Because I myself experienced it. Many times. Here's an example. Remember how, at the start of the Covid pandemic, they sold out of many foodstuffs. Because everyone was panic-buying. One of them was bog-standard easy-cook brown rice. But they still had this bewildering array of other, fancy, types. Just looking at them made my head spin, and I was unable to decide which one to choose.

> No, it isn't very nice:
> All I wanted was brown rice,
> But the shelves had been stripped bare:
> I've gone hunting everywhere.

Now, what would be your advice?
How do I procure brown rice?

No, I wanted nothing fancy,
Yet my quest had proved quite chancy:
They did have some black and wild,
When I saw the bag, I smiled.

Even if you up the price,
I must purchase some brown rice.

As for jasmine, cream or puffed,
They might just as well get stuffed.
Boil-in-bag or gluten-free?
Coconut? Please hear my plea:

I just can't be more precise:
All I want is some brown rice.

Just one bag of decent size
Will suffice, I promise, guys:
Brown, bog-standard, easy-cook –
I don't want a fancy look.

It is my undoubted vice,
But I won't consume white rice…

And this forest-whole – who knew
That rice grew in forests too?
Red indica, Taiwanese?
Too much choice: just stop it, please!

Chilli, spicy, sweet? No dice:
I desire my brown rice.

And this Mexican inspired?
Gosh, I'm growing really tired,
And my smile is rather wry:
What's it been inspired by?

Please don't make me say this twice:
Nothing beats my plain brown rice.

Let me just reiterate:
I am not at all au fait
With all this superior stuff:
Brown, bog-standard is enough.

I won't give it to the mice;
Please just sell me some brown rice!

Look, this rice is certified;
I don't think that I can hide
My spontaneous urge to yell:
"I will shortly be as well!"

Maybe that's why I have developed this certifiable urge to climb every Lakeland fell in sight and then to keep doing this again and again; I will get to this bit soon. Another strategy for dealing with an abundance of choice is simply to give in and grab everything in sight. Remember the run on loo rolls? I mean, also at the start of the pandemic. This was such an essential item that Vinnie and I simply decided to follow the crowd. When in Rome…

We are on a wartime footing:
Thankfully, there's been no looting,
But we need a huge supply
Of loo rolls; we want four-ply,

Perfumed, plush and medicated
(Though their merits are debated);
Triple satin would be good,
And we also think we should

Get a lot of quilted ones;
Yep, we're certain to need tons.
Ultra-soft or ultra-strong?
We don't want to get this wrong,

So it's best to get them both;
You are doubtful? On my oath!
Finger-breakthrough is an issue
With some types of bathroom tissue,

Ergo our fierce insistence
On their absolute resistance,
And absorption also matters;
As regards spontaneous splatters…

No, perhaps it's better not
Dwelling on this very thought.
Anyway, let's get a truck –
Here is hoping for some luck.

At the store, our cool mask slips:
This is an apocalypse!
Crowds are storming at the shelves:
What are we to do ourselves?

The dilemma has hit home,
Then again, when one's in Rome…
So we join the throng and grasp
All the packs that fit our clasp:

Andrex, Angel Soft, Cushelle,
Nicky, Charmin, Naturelle,
Kleenex, Panda, Caprice Green –
Various brands on which one's keen.

Without being too specific:
All those products are terrific,
Keeping our, let's say, flesh
Quite pristine and garden-fresh.

What? You're saying it's inglorious?
But our quest has been victorious!
So when we, at last, depart,
We feel provident and smart.

After we have stashed the haul
Propping it against each wall,
There's a shout – it is my spouse:
"We will need a bigger house!"

But where was I? Oh, yes: bucket list. I'm sure you won't be surprised that I subsequently discovered the true meaning of this phrase. But the concept seemed as weird as this list for different buckets. We didn't have anything like this in the communist Poland of my youth: everyone was too preoccupied with getting from one pay cheque to the next to even consider such an indulgence. But I was now in the affluent West, so this was another peculiar thing I had to get accustomed to. Not that I *myself* have ever succumbed to the slightest desire to ape the lovely natives. Why? After all, I have found my Lakeland paradise, so why would I want to go traipsing around the world in search of so-called experiences?

> If you're someone, you'll insist
> On a fancy bucket list;
> If you make it very long,
> It might help you get the gong.
>
> I'm a minnow, though, so I
> Have the licence not to try;
> Plus, I cherish calm and peace –
> It's a feeling that won't cease.
>
> You might have just what it takes –
> I'm ensconced in our Lakes,
> Where, in a reflective mood,
> I delight in solitude.

Fancy Iceland's Blue Lagoon?
That's not what would make *me* swoon:
I'm so grateful to be here,
Feeding ducks in Buttermere.

Bungee jumping off the Shard?
It would leave me deeply scarred,
As the only jumps I do
Are those dodging livestock's poo.

Machu Picchu is your aim?
My ambition's rather tame:
Lakeland's lofty trails to tread
And return to my own bed.

Planning rafting up the Nile?
It may take you quite a while;
I would choose the picturesque
And delightful River Esk.

If your latest urgent whim
Is to have a playful swim
With black dolphins, I would like
Merely to observe a pike.

Taj Mahal will be your next?
Such long flights would leave me vexed:
I prefer St Beda's Church,
Shaded by a native birch.

> You might think that I'm a bore,
> That I should hold out for more,
> But my life is *far* from bland:
> I live in a foreign land!

And, in my Lakeland paradise, I have had enough adventures to satisfy a few lifetimes – and to fill more books. I hope that my account of the escapades and mishaps featuring in this one will at least give you the flavour of what I have experienced in the spellbinding Lake District over the past quarter of the century. So why would I want to go in search of excitement elsewhere? Particularly abroad. All the hassle of packing and unpacking, the former invariably entailing missing at least one absolutely essential item; enduring train delays and cancellations; ditto with planes, with the additional attraction of being swamped by a mass of irritated humanity which, like you, has already been waiting for eleven hours to take to the skies; being exposed to ear-shattering screams of some unfortunate baby in the seat immediately in front of yours for the entire duration of your nine-hour flight; being forced to breathe in the fumes given off by a pack of heavily inebriated guys off to a stag weekend; being struck by travel sickness en route to your overseas destination; getting grotesquely overcharged by a foreign taxi driver who drives you to your hotel while you are suffering from severe jet lag; finding your accommodation far inferior to that advertised in terms of its visual appeal, size, position, layout, view, Wi-Fi connectivity and cleanliness (could these really be bed bugs?); being dismayed that the natives don't speak your language; getting lost on your first foray into the foreign territory; getting mugged during the aforementioned foray; discovering that what you have actually ordered at a restaurant is like nothing you thought you were ordering; being bitten by foreign insects, whose sting is far worse than that of the home variety; losing your smartphone, without which your life grinds to a shuddering halt; suffering sunburn, heat exhaustion or heatstroke (maybe even all three in concert); and contracting traveller's diarrhoea swiftly followed by an E. coli infection, neither of which, you subsequently find, is covered by your cut-price travel insurance – to name but a few irritants of international travel. If you are really lucky, of course, you will be turned away at border control because you have less than three months left on your passport, but not everyone can enjoy such good fortune.

And, because Vinnie and I don't travel, our blood pressure never rises above 110 over 70 – *never*, so our GP has given us a gold star each. Besides, we pride ourselves on our modest carbon footprint, of which more later. But I think I had better rewind: after all, I haven't told you yet how I made it from Poland to Britain – let alone to the Lake District.

2

From the Polish Tatras to the English Lakes

But I'm too young to die, I panicked as my arms and legs began to give way. I was clinging to a vertiginous rock face desperately trying to pull myself over a seemingly insurmountable obstacle: an overhang in the form of a rough crag looming immediately above. My arms were aching, and my legs began to shake uncontrollably: I was stuck. No, I must try again! Somehow, I managed to heave my body over the edge of the crag and, having cleared the hurdle, collapsed on easier ground, shaking and terrified. True, I was roped up, but, in those days in Poland, we didn't have proper climbing harnesses. Instead, we simply tied a rope around our chest and hoped for the best. Surely, if I had fallen off, the rope would have crushed my ribs. Thankfully, I never got to put the theory to the test, deciding there and then that I wasn't going to be God's gift to rock climbing. I was seventeen years old and had become bewitched by the

Tatra Mountains (we call them Tatry in Poland) a mere three years previously.

I'm sure you could Google the Tatras (how the human race managed to cope before Google I know not), but I may as well tell you that they are a spectacularly beautiful mountain range in southern Poland, the highest within the Western Carpathians. Though they are smaller than the Alps, their landscape is strikingly similar, the High Tatras in particular soaring into the sky in a dramatic series of jagged peaks. When, while still at school, I spent my first summer holiday in Zakopane, a Polish equivalent of Cumbrian Keswick, Grasmere or Ambleside, I got well and truly hooked. Although my subsequent foray into climbing was brief, it was back then that my passion for fell-walking took hold. A hold which hasn't lessened in the course of the following several decades and which has me in its iron grip to this day.

In those days, Poland was in the clutches of the Soviet Union, having been ceded by the West to the evil Soviet empire after the Second World War. The Iron Curtain having descended in the middle of Europe, separating it into the free West and the enslaved East, we had no access to western countries, and I had no inkling that, one day, I would end up in Britain. Despite this, I studied English assiduously, English grammar in particular becoming my all-consuming passion.

Anyway, end up in Britain I did after General Jaruzelski imposed martial law on our country in order to forestall a threatened Soviet invasion. Our borders were thus sealed off and I was shut out, for I was already in Britain to take several advanced qualifications in English in order to complement my two university degrees (in Poland, I had been teaching English). You see, despite the considerable travelling restrictions imposed on us by our communist masters, a slight relaxation had slowly started to creep in, and it had become possible for us Poles to head west, although it certainly wasn't easy. But, before I could travel, I had to obtain sufficient funds to support myself in Britain. I was thus saving every last penny to buy American dollars – on the black market, naturally. In communist countries (or, more precisely, in countries such as Poland, on which communism had been forcibly and brutally imposed against their will by the Russia-dominated Soviet federation), it was forbidden to have any western currency: after all, the West was our mortal enemy and anything having any connection with it was contaminated, at least according to the communist propaganda with which we were being systematically indoctrinated (ultimately, unsuccessfully: we weren't that stupid). With no official exchange rate, you had to pay whatever cost the dealer decided you could bear; after all, those enterprising people were putting themselves at risk by bringing the illegal dosh into the country.

So here I was at the airport about to board a London-bound plane. But, before I could take to the skies, I had to undergo the customary frisking by our diligent customs officers. The Cerberus wanted to see what was in my handbag, so, trembling, I opened it and handed it over to her. But before she got hold of it, I managed to take out my purse and stood there, petrified, the purse in my outstretched hand: inside were the forbidden dollars.

Inexplicably ignoring the purse right in front of her nose, she rummaged through my bag and, having found nothing of interest to the authorities, handed it back to me. As she was doing so, she gave me a quizzical look, asking why I was so nervous. Nervous? Who? *Me?* I affected astonishment while, at the same time, trying to conceal the purse in the now sanitised bag. But she had obviously decided that she might have better luck with another victim – I mean traveller – and let me go. They should have trained them better, but the crazy system had so impoverished the economy that they must have run out of money for proper surveillance. If she had found the verboten hard currency, I would undoubtedly have had to kiss my dreams of visiting the West goodbye. Who knows, I might have even ended up in prison. After all, they were imprisoning people on the flimsiest of excuses – or without any excuses at all. They were the absolute rulers, our so-called communism being no more than a form of dictatorship brutally imposed on us by the imperialist Russia.

Obviously, Britain wasn't too keen on letting any Tom, Dick and Harry in either, but, when your border guards were on a cigarette break, I managed to sneak into London a couple of times before embarking on my fateful sojourn. (You should have policed your borders better. Then again, maybe Poland and Britain were not so different in this particular respect, after all.) What a contrast! I found London intoxicating and baffling in equal measure, criss-crossing the metropolis whenever I could, astonished by the stark dissimilarity between the two countries. But I wasn't idle and quickly laid a foundation stone under my professional career – initially, as a broadcaster at the Polish Section of the BBC. I then swerved, somewhat violently, to education, running public examinations, developing national qualifications, copy editing and penning articles and books on my favourite topic: English grammar, punctuation and usage. Thus I toiled until, in my mid-forties, I was walloped by a full-blown mid-life crisis: the daily grind of office work, combined with a tiresome commute, was beginning to take its toll, as well as the frenzied pace of metropolitan life, which had gradually lost its initial sheen.

The green light shone when Vinnie managed to bag a very early retirement – at fifty-one! I was too young to follow suit, but, where there is a will, there is a way. We thus crossed our fingers, packed up our London house and headed north, to the stunning Lake District, chanced upon by me some ten years previously. While not the Tatras, Lakeland had its own breathtaking beauty, which enchanted and ensnared me as soon as I laid my eyes on it.

So there we were, in the delightful market town of Keswick, embarking on a brand-new adventure. Why Keswick? Well, we are rather atypical in that neither of us drives. The reason is quite simple: neither of us has ever *learnt* to drive, so it might have been rather foolhardy for either to attempt to get behind the wheel. Which is what we would have needed to do had we chosen to live in some enchanting cottage in the middle of an equally enchanting nowhere. As non-drivers, we thus needed to drop anchor somewhere where we could pop out for an emergency pint of milk without relying on a vehicle, and Keswick fitted the bill perfectly. And, of course, the town is surrounded by fells – a walker's paradise.

Admittedly, being unable to drive while living in the Lakes could be a bit of a bugger for someone who was hell-bent on exploring every last nook and cranny, and on climbing each and every mountain, hill and knoll, in this enchanted land. But one ought to look on the bright side: it has provided one with endless material for one's books, so one can't complain.

So, having landed in Keswick – hold on, I think I've said something about dropping anchor, so imagine us in our new harbour – we have had a marvellous time getting to know all its delights and idiosyncrasies. Suddenly, we look back, and it's been over a quarter of a century! And it is from this vantage point that I have been able to compose this paean to our lovely little town.

> Years ago, we settled down
> In this lovely little town,
> Which, and that's beyond dispute,
> Is as pretty as it's cute.
>
> There is something here for all:
> We have got a climbing wall,
> Nice old churches and (you've guessed)
> Pubs for that deserved, hmmm… rest,
>
> And, of course, refreshing beer
> In a vibrant atmosphere,
> Whiskeys, vodkas, wines galore:
> You've had some, you'll beg for more.

If you'd rather not have vino,
They will serve you cappuccino,
Moka, miel and other kinds –
Good for energising minds.

We have caffs – and every one
Used to guarantee good fun;
Now, however, we're bereft:
Nearly all the staff have left.

If, though, you want outdoor gear,
Forty shops are very near;
Strictly speaking, we do not
Need as many as we've got,

But I won't be a dissenter:
We are an adventure centre.
As for the accommodation,
It's the envy of this nation:

Our comfy B&Bs
Never, ever fail to please,
And, if you should wish to camp,
Glamping pods will have no damp,

While our worldly clientele
Will adore each plush hotel –
The embodiment of swank,
And we even had a bank!

Though its hours had been cut,
No-one thought that it would shut,
Then, suddenly, it was gone:
We all felt it was a con.

But we have retained such gems
As three handy ATMs;
Two of them are often busted,
But the other can be trusted.

What is more, we prize our stake
In the Theatre By The Lake
And Alhambra, where each movie
Is inevitably groovy.

Our parks? Another asset,
Although, if you own a Bassett
Or another pooch, don't sin:
Drop the poo bag in the bin.

That aside, in all those places
We see lots of friendly faces,
So, we think – and think we do –
It's a real dream come true.

What is more, our eyes can binge
On the fells that Keswick fringe –
Sparkling jewels in the crown
Of this lovely little town.

Yep, it was (and, most happily, still is) our own little paradise. Imagine walking out of your front door and being able to climb a mountain – or two (or even three). And to do lots of marvellous walks throughout the Lake District while using public transport. This is also why we don't travel. Why would we want to bother when we have all this breathtaking beauty right on our doorstep? Besides, our modest carbon footprint is good for the planet. And I live in a foreign country anyway, so don't talk to me about the desirability of exposure to other cultures. You won't believe the gymnastics I have had to perform to try to shed my otherness. Regrettably, however, it continues to stick like discarded chewing gum to the sole of one's shoe. If you are adventurous enough to persevere with this book, you will see what I mean.

In a different vein, whenever one tries to express oneself in verse, as I often do, one needs a muse. My own Lady Muse (the current one is British; I've had to retire the Polish one), usually exasperated with me for failing to reach her exacting standard, sporadically makes a Herculean effort, grabbing me by the scuff of the neck and trying to drag me up. It was on one of those, regrettably rare, occasions that I penned the verse below. Sadly, I crashed back down pretty quickly, as you will undoubtedly soon discover.

> Yesterday, I took a stroll
> Up a most delightful knoll,
> Which, though dwarfed by bigger brothers,
> Offers views unmatched by others.

There I sat, quite pensive, and,
With the chin upon my hand,
Looked across the glistening vale
At the Jaws of Borrowdale.

There was stillness all around,
With no movement and no sound,
As I watched the sun slip down
In a distant lake to drown.

While I marvelled in delight
At the nature's spell and might,
I felt humble, I felt small,
Undeserving of it all,
And the air stood very still
On this lovely little hill.

3

My First Lakeland Fiasco

So here we were: Vinnie, my elderly mum (who had joined us, initially in London, in the early nineties) and I contentedly ensconced in our comfortable Lakeland house, although our garage didn't appear too happy to be stacked with unpacked boxes rather than being able to bathe in the refined fragrance naturally given off by a swanky Jaguar Land Rover, Maserati, Volvo, Mercedes-Benz or, indeed, Lexus LM. Although, in our case, it would probably have been some clapped-out old Trabant. No matter, we were never going to live up to our garage's lofty aspirations.

What's this obsession with cars, anyway? We didn't need one. After all, there was no commuting to work: Vinnie was retired, and I had set up a home-based educational consultancy, so work was coming to me. Which rather fills me with pride, my being ahead of the working-from-home curve; usually, I am well and truly behind every trend going. True, I had to attend quite a lot of meetings in London, Glasgow and Edinburgh, but I always let the train take the strain. And, to use local amenities, we simply walked into town. Or hopped on the bus (riding on the top deck, where there is one, can be great fun). And, of course, buses (and, occasionally, local trains, boats and ferries) were my gateway to the magnificent Lake District fells, which I was dying to explore. I soon worked out that the local buses could deliver one to lots of lovely places, particularly if one planned one's connections cleverly. Thus began my quest to scale all Lake District fells, large, medium and small, a feat which I have now managed to accomplish many times over.

Actually, I've climbed every one of them at least nine times and am currently finishing my tenth round. After all, I can't be outdone by Fred, can I?

> "Nine rounds of Wainwrights!" she would boast,
> Thinking she'd done by far the most;
> Fred gave her a stare:
> "I've done ten, so there!"
> It was *he* whom the Roamers did toast…

The Roamers are a local walking group led by me, but we have a little way to go before I introduce them to you properly. Well worth waiting for, though.

As for our inability to drive, whenever one of us mentioned this fact, we were met with a mixture of pity and incredulity. Eventually, it started to grate, and I decided to take the plunge: when in Rome… oops, I've already used this phrase. Note to self: don't mention Rome again. I can only hope that I will be able to stick with my resolution more successfully than John Cleese did with his intent never to mention the war.

Anyway, I hired this driving instructor, a fellow Keswickian, and my lessons began. What an unmitigated disaster! How anybody can drive along those narrow winding Cumbrian roads is beyond me. The experience was so traumatic that prose simply fails me. Which is why I have captured my motoring ordeal in verse.

> They all said, "If you don't drive,
> Life is harder: you can't thrive."
> Yet I'd always done quite well:
> "I *am* thriving, can't you tell?"
>
> They, however, would not stop,
> Even if I threw a strop,
> So the seed of doubt was sown:
> Should I leave my car-free zone?
>
> After it had taken root,
> This idea seemed astute:
> Me behind a wheel, yippee!
> I would be completely free.
>
> They all knew this pleasant chap
> Who would never, ever flap
> When instructing learners, so
> I resolved to have a go.

We thus started, Dom and I –
He *was* quite a patient guy;
To begin with, it was fun –
Serious mishaps? Almost none,

Although I could never learn
How to do a three-point turn,
And, when hitting on the brake,
I would almost always quake:

It was (I am still a hater)
Next to the accelerator!
We continued; then there came
Time for me to up my game,

So we headed into town:
There were lots of folk around;
Now, what do I go and do?
Mount the pavement – it is true!

This poor bloke, he had to jump
To escape with just a bump,
At which point, Dom takes a swig
From a bottle (not that big).

I don't want to sound Shakespearean,
But this potion was Valerian.
Anyway, we then proceed
To experiment with speed;

We got to this busy road,
So I, naturally, slowed,
Plus, the car was not that sporty,
Which is why I drove at forty.

And what happens? They all beep:
This Ford Fiesta and this jeep,
And the bloody rest; how vile,
Not to mention juvenile.

Those two fingers in the air
Reinforcing hostile glare –
All this made me rather drawn,
But I bravely soldiered on,

Although slowing to a crawl
When I saw a great big wall,
While this lorry, I could see,
Headed straight, head-on, at me.

Which collision would be worse?
Although each would be a curse,
Anything that sits quite still
May be less inclined to kill,

So I chose the wall, but Dom,
With great coolness and aplomb,
Shoved me quickly to one side,
Halting our hairy ride.

Two more swigs and up he perks:
This Valerian clearly works.
Soon, he's at his very best,
Helping me progress my quest.

We are at this roundabout –
All that traffic! So I shout
And then quickly shut my eyes:
One can't witness one's demise.

Then I feel a great big swerve:
Dominic, with all his verve,
Yanks the steering wheel; oh gosh –
That's how you avoid a squash.

Although he was quite a dude,
At that point I did conclude
That, whatever they may say,
Driving wasn't a child's play.

So I did decide to quit;
He rejoiced, the hypocrite
(Of this, I had not a hunch),
Then he toasted with rum punch!

Well, I certainly wasn't cut out for getting behind the wheel, that's for sure. And the world has undoubtedly been spared its worst ever driver. Besides, if the acclaimed author A. Wainwright could get around by public transport, so jolly well could I! And our garage was given a new lease of life, having been converted into my office, badly needed for my consultancy work, linguistic research and writing – both scholarly and jocular, the latter not only predominating but also often hijacking the former, humour being in my DNA. But we also have a redundant drive and are very pleased whenever we can offer it to our wonderful neighbours, Carol and Nicky: you have to cultivate good neighbours, you know. As far as Vinnie and I are concerned, they are worth their weight in rhodium (you can look rhodium up on Google).

> A good neighbour's hard to find;
> We have two: each very kind –
> Lovely Carol, helpful Nicky,
> It is really very tricky
> To express how we both feel:
> Look, the pair's the real deal!

4

Upstaging Princess Anne and the Keswick Lift Incident

Pensioner Trapped in Lift, screamed the headline on the front page. Pensioner? I did a double take. *Me?* But I was a strong, fit and healthy (apart from my dodgy hip, of which later) – not to mention youthful (albeit, admittedly, only on the inside) – fell walker and mountain guide, each week covering some forty or so miles scaling Lakeland heights (although, in my heyday, I could easily manage twice that). How could I be a pensioner, with all the negative connotations of the designation? But the reality was inescapable: technically, I was one. And right there, in the middle of the page, was my photograph, with my name underneath it, accompanied by a florid description of my lift ordeal. Actually, the floridity (one of these fancy words which definitely exist) had come from me: how else would they have become aware of the immensity of my torment?

Actually, I had been itching to get you started on my carless Lakeland adventures but suddenly realised that

I couldn't – not before revealing that Keswick boasted (and, thankfully, still does) another marvellous institution, namely its own newspaper, *The Keswick Reminder*. Can you imagine? A town of barely 5,000 inhabitants (although it feels more like a million in the tourist season) having its own weekly. Amazing! First published in 1896, *The Reminder* has served its local community in a most excellent fashion all this time and is beloved by us all. Needless to say, purchasing it every Friday morning has been something of a ritual ever since we moved here. I have a particular reason to be loyal to it, for it regularly publishes my jazzy articles about the mountain walks I lead for my lovely Roamers (whom I mentioned in the previous chapter). The group operates under the auspices of the u3a, which stands for the University of the Third Age. A bit later, I will tell you more about the u3a, for it's a fantastic worldwide movement for those who have entered their third, vintage, age.

Returning to *The Keswick Reminder*, its kindness in publishing my articles pales into insignificance in comparison with the fact that the paper gave me my greatest claim to fame – a claim so humongous that, whatever else I contrive to achieve on this Earth, nothing could surely better it: my lift-incident story had displaced an article on Princess Anne's visit to the Lake District, relegating it to the back page of *The Reminder*. So here I am, right at the front, while Her Royal Highness had been unceremoniously shoved to the back – how do you trump *that*?

Anyway, I've probably kept you in suspense for long enough, so here is the story. One consequence of being as rare as hen's teeth in a country which considers having at least one car per person (ideally, with a second one for spare) to be a fundamental human right is that one needs a shopping trolley. (Come to think of it, Maslow's hierarchy of needs ought to be extended to include a car alongside air, food, water, sex, sleep and other basic physiological needs.) To the likes of me, a shopping trolley is thus indispensable. Mine, of a sleek design and funky appearance, is rarely parted from me, and I wheel it around exuberantly. Actually, Vinnie has a matching one, so when we go shopping, people stop and gawp. But he is a New Man, not feeling in the least emasculated by his cart. Give me a man secure in his masculinity any day is what I say.

> They all cry: "Oh gosh, oh golly!"
> When I'm shopping with my trolley;
> It's so roomy and so cool,
> If you saw it, you would drool.
>
> There's no doubt it's right on trend,
> My eye-catching shopping friend,
> And it's got a snazzy twin
> Gamely carted by my Vin:
>
> Though his temples may be grey,
> He's a New Man – yippee yay!
> So, in fact, there's four of us
> In the street and on the bus.
>
> But it isn't how they look
> That's our trolleys' greatest hook,
> For we get a real thrill
> From their carbon footprint: nil!

Yep, with our Earth-friendly lifestyle, I reckon we could even start flogging carbon credits – at a reasonable price, of course.

Anyway, it was to my stripy Rolser that I had entrusted some books and other reading matter and was now carting them to our council offices on that fateful day. I needed the stuff for one of Gill's marvellous creative writing workshops, run under the aegis of our equally marvellous Skiddaw u3a. These workshops were held in the grand Council Chamber and attended by several of my fellow lady pensioners. And I was about to join the delightful group, who, judging by the chatter emanating from above, had already gathered in the aforementioned assembly room, situated on the first floor.

The load in my trolley was rather heavy, and one thing a laden trolley doesn't like is being dragged up the stairs, so there was only one thing for it – the lift, an invention nearly as mind-blowing as the trolley itself. Even though I rarely take lifts, I summoned this one unhesitatingly, stepped in boldly and pressed the up-button – somewhat nonchalantly. The machine creaked, shook and commenced its upward crawl. As we inched towards the first floor, I marvelled at this ancient piece of engineering and wondered whether it would qualify for a listed status – grade C, maybe? As I was pondering if a lift could actually be listed as an object of special architectural or historic interest, the thing came to a gentle stop. I grabbed my trolley and moved towards the door – only to find that there was *no* door.

I stood there, startled: *where the hell has it gone?* I looked around, but all I could see were walls – on all *four* sides. Good grief! I looked up, and there it was, a sliver of light at the very bottom of the door. But it was way above my head; even on tiptoe, I couldn't reach it. *How? Why? What the…?* I looked around my trap: the only thing I could do – apart from screaming, obviously – was to press the buttons. One was the down-button, one was the up-button, one was the panic button, and one was the stop button. Well, I certainly didn't need *that* one! I pressed the up-button with all the force I could muster – nothing. I frantically pressed the down-button – not a thing.

The next logical thing to do was to scream at the top of my lungs, at which point it occurred to me that the panic button could also come in handy. Granted, pressing it didn't offer any *practical* solution, but both actions produced the desired effect: after a spell of my hollering from the depths of the lift shaft, reinforced with the sound of the alarm bell, an unfamiliar female chin appeared high up in the small window positioned at the top of the lift door. The possessor of the chin, probably a female council clerk, peered down.

"Have you pressed the button?"

Have I pressed the button?! Never in the history of button-pressing has there been a more concerted effort expended on pressing the damn thing.

"I have, I have, look!" I yelled and repeated the manoeuvre in a most demonstrative way I was capable of. The chin wobbled, which probably meant that its owner nodded, and disappeared from view. I could hear footsteps echoing in the free world and then some sort of commotion. Then, a black beard materialised high up. I waved, rather pathetically.

"Have you pressed the button?"

Have I…? "Yes, yes, look!"

Reassured that I had, indeed, pressed the button in question, the beard performed a similar wobbling motion, its possessor saying, "We'll get you somebody."

"Maybe the fire brigade?"

The beard disappeared, and I could hear more noises. A female voice, this one clearly belonging to one of my fellow lady pensioners, was pondering the practicalities of using a crowbar in similar circumstances, with others making contributions I couldn't quite catch, although somebody did mention a ladder. Now was the time to appraise my predicament more coolly, if coolly could be applied to what was in effect an increasingly stuffy cage. I examined my trap again. How far was it to the bottom of the door – five/six feet, perhaps? So, after they have smashed the door, they would have to lower a ladder to get me out. How many rungs would that be? Now, I have a confession to make: although I have scaled innumerable mountains, I'm no good with ladders and turn to jelly after the first few steps. But, somehow, I didn't think I would be a reluctant ladder-climber on this particular occasion and began to feel slightly better.

"Are they coming?" I yelled.

A female voice from above said, "Some council bloke is."

"*What* council bloke?"

"From Workington."

"From Workington? But it's miles away – with the parking and that, it may take an hour!"

"No, no, they said twelve minutes."

"*But you can't get from Workington to Keswick in twelve minutes! It's twenty-three miles!*"

"No, no, they definitely said twelve minutes. Have you pressed the button?"

"*Y-e-e-e-s!*"

My exasperation with this line of questioning notwithstanding, I felt that, if they *definitely* said twelve minutes, further arguments would be futile. Besides, I wasn't exactly in a strong bargaining position, although – with hindsight – I could have feigned a faint or something. But people of my moral rectitude don't pull stunts like that. The only thing at this juncture was to relieve tension by cracking manic jokes, and I believe I started demanding that my rescuers be handsome and making other similarly inappropriate comments. Gallows humour, they call it – I can certainly see what they mean.

After more than half an hour, however, even this strategy began to show cracks.

"May I have the fire brigade, please?"

"He's coming, he's coming!"

"The fire brigade?"

"No, they are not allowed to call the fire brigade."

"*Who* is not allowed?"

"The council."

"*Whyever* not?"

"Because they may have to pay."

Jeez, so I could expire here for the sake of a few measly quid! The outside world was baking in oppressive heat as it was, so you can imagine how stifling my prison was.

"*Please, please, get me the fire brigade!*"

"Not long now, not long now. But we've found the manual!"

Now, lady pensioners are incontrovertibly a pillar

of the community, but the image of them holding the manual with one hand while, with the other, fiddling with lift electrics – or was it electronics? – somehow failed to offer me the reassurance I so desperately needed at that juncture. Were any of them into electrics – or was it electronics? – at all? I knew for a fact that one was into birdwatching and another into enamelling, but I wondered about the others. Wait, wait, one said she was in the Women's Institute! Didn't somebody tell me once that the WI was supposed to have made great strides since the days of jam-making and was now into all sorts? But could they have possibly progressed so far? I mean, providing women with educational opportunities is one thing, but actually branching out into engineering…?

"*Fire brigade!*" I wailed in a voice I barely recognised.

"Won't be long, won't be long. But you know what?"

"*What? What?*"

"Apparently, they serviced the lift last week."

Heavens above, was our local government is such dire financial straits that they couldn't stretch to half-decent lift maintenance? If so, we were surely all doomed, this refrain from a well-known British film racing through my mind. But the thought of my own impending doom was far more pressing.

"*Get me the fire brigade!*"

"He'll be here in a minute!"

An hour into my imprisonment, I heard some loud banging and then another male voice.

"It may be the fuse," said the male voice. Now, I defy anybody who denies men their uses.

"*This* fuse?" My lady pensioners were clearly on the ball.

I heard some more noises, and then, out of the blue, the light in the lift went out. *What the…?*

"I'm sorry, I'm sorry, I should have warned you," said the male voice.

So he should have, but at least he was apologetic.

"I'll let you know before I turn it off again."

"Please do," I wailed.

He did, but no amount of fiddling with the electrics – or was it electronics? – could bring the lift back to life. There was further banging and shaking, there were further footsteps and confabulations, but I still wasn't going anywhere.

It was now an hour and a half into my ordeal, and, to make matters even worse, I could no longer hear the male voice.

"*Call the fire brigade, please!*"

"We are calling the fire brigade."

Did I hear this right? It looked as if the lady pensioners had taken matters into their own hands – at long last! The fire brigade arrived within a few minutes. When it appeared high up in the little window, the first male chin, with a helmet just about discernible above, was a vision to relish. The boys set to work immediately. Amid much noise, the lift began shaking violently and then, inch by inch, making its slow descent to the floor below. Suddenly, a portion of a little window appeared at the very bottom of the lift. I crouched and, instead of chins, I could now see helmets, then foreheads, then eyes, then noses, then lips and then entire faces. And I could hear lots of excited chatter, for, in anticipation of my imminent release, the entire congregation had relocated to the lower floor. And then, I was free. Needless to say, the firefighters were the handsomest men I had ever set my eyes on!

My trolley is brilliant – I love it so much;
I gathered some books (they made quite a clutch)
And put them inside – the wheels took the strain,
But what they don't like are stairs – in the main.

A lift is thus handy, and that's what I took –
It creaked and it spluttered, it whined and it shook;
We got to our floor, but… there was no door!
The number of walls? By Jove, there were four!

I took a deep breath, looked round and could see
That there was no way for me to break free;
There were, though, four buttons: one *up* and one *stop*,
One *down* and one *panic* – tried all: 'twas a flop.

I screamed, then looked up: a slither of light
High up – near the ceiling – a most welcome sight;
A chin then appeared; its owner did peer
At me at the bottom, thus easing my fear.

"You pressed the right button?" the chin asked me then;
"I have, I *have* done!" I did it again.
"Hmm, this is quite strange." The chin disappeared.
I waited a while and saw a black beard.

"You pressed the right button?" its owner did ask;
"I *have*, but no joy!" My face a grim mask.
"Hmm, this is quite strange." The beard was no more,
And then, at the top, a guy yelled and swore.

"Please, get me," I wailed, "the fire brigade!"
My trap was quite hot, and I was afraid.
"Will get you somebody, don't worry, don't fret:
A bloke from the council." I started to sweat.

"A bloke from the council?" (The building was theirs,
And so was the lift: they did the repairs.)
"He won't be that long – twelve minutes at max."
I have to admit this made me relax.

Twelve minutes did pass, then thirty – no show,
And I was, again, quite frightened and low.
"The fire brigade!" I pleaded anew,
Then heard, higher up, a hullabaloo.

"They will not let us!" "Who won't? Who are 'they'?"
"The council." "But why?" "They may have to pay."
My life had no worth? It hit me, this thought;
I stood there distressed, upset, overwrought.

The girls I was meeting, they all gathered round,
And Betty exclaimed, "Look what I've just found:
We might fix the lift!" (A manual, then?)
I took a deep breath and counted to ten:

These ladies, my friends, are all OAPs,
And there is so much they handle with ease,
But *lift maintenance*? *Electrics*? No way!
I stifled a sob and started to pray.

At long last, result: this bloke had appeared:
The banging he did – it sounded so weird;
He said, "I don't know, it may be the fuse,"
The light then went out; I shouted abuse.

"I'm sorry, I'm sorry!" the idiot exclaimed.
Why didn't he warn me? He should be ashamed.
"*The fire brigade, the fire brigade!*"
My hope was, by now, beginning to fade.

Ignoring the council, my Gill (she's so fine)
Got hold of her mobile and dialled 999;
I soon saw some chins – and helmets above –
And now comprehend the meaning of love.

The boys set to work, the lift got the shakes –
By Jove, those brave guys have got what it takes.
It may well have been a sluggish descent,
But it put an end to this vile event.

Those boys, I must tell you, so handsome and fine
Are all, to the last one, great heroes of mine;
And if I were younger and prettier and sporty…
Some twenty years younger – oh gosh, make it forty!

It would seem that, on occasion, excitement can be found quite close to home, but I'd much rather experience it on the fells. Which brings me to my Lakeland exploits – or should I say, mishaps and lunacies. But, if you should ever find yourself in need of a face-to-face confabulation with a council official, it might be an idea to use the stairs, what with all the swingeing cuts to local authority budgets.

5

Getting about in the Lakes and the Dale Head Mishap

We live in a car-owning democracy, which, however, has its own drawbacks. In the provinces, you are often stuffed without a car. Which isn't good for the planet.

> This pronouncement isn't trite:
> Our freedom is our right;
> One, however, won't get far
> Until one procures a car.
>
> Local buses? Most have gone,
> This heralding a new dawn;
> Dr Beeching killed our trains,
> It's an auto that thus reigns;
>
> Demos consequently feels
> A desire for four wheels;
> Fair enough, but what I say

> To those folk who do hold sway:
> Do re-think and, changing tack,
> Give us public transport back!

When he was writing his now mega-famous seven guides on the 214 main Lakeland fells, Alfred Wainwright would get about by public transport. Not sure how he would fare now. It's funny: you keep telling people for decades that, without a car, they don't amount to much, and then, when everybody gets one (at the very least), thus giving you licence to decimate provincial buses and trains, you tell them to ditch it and get on their bike. Or use horse and cart, like in the olden days, there being no other viable alternatives. But much of Wainwright's life was spent before Margaret Thatcher declared Britain a car-owning democracy, and exploring the Lakes by public transport was probably a tad easier for him back then.

To be fair, the service I was using in the late nineties and early noughties wasn't bad at all. We had these nimble, subsidised, buses which, in high season, would deliver you to far-away places such as Burnbanks, Mardale Head, Howtown, Newby Bridge, Bowness Knott and even Ennerdale Bridge. With careful planning, which inevitably involved combining different modes of transport, one could even reach Wasdale Head, Eskdale and the west coast – if one was prepared to spend up to seven hours in transit, which, like a person possessed, I was.

For a few precious years, instrumental in my reaching the far south and the far west was this fabulous X33, which ran on Saturdays and Sundays in the summer season all the way from Penrith to Ravenglass via Keswick, Coniston and Broughton in Furness and then past Silecroft and Muncaster Castle. Of course, if you missed the return bus on a Sunday, you would be stranded until the following Saturday, and I certainly had my fair share of near-misses (as well as the actual ones).

But then the government decided to waste – I mean spend – billions and billions of pounds on the HS2 and other grand schemes to ensure that Britain became world-beating at absolutely everything. The way Boris Johnson enunciated the phrase 'world beating, *yes, world-beating*' – both before and after he became World King, I mean Prime Minister – swelled our chests with immense pride. I say 'our' advisedly, for, ever since I settled in this great country, I have made strenuous efforts to assimilate, integrate and blend. I hope that, by the end of this book, you will be able to judge the extent to which my efforts have borne fruit. But, please, be gentler than Kian. You see, I had tried and tried *and tried* to earn the coveted badge of an upstanding British citizen, even becoming a voluntary walk leader, giving selflessly of my time to brighten others' day. I've already told you about the Roamers. Twice. And among my flock is Kian, who is going to make an appearance in the verse below.

But there was more to my efforts at obtaining a nationality transplant: I also wrote a book on English grammar, punctuation and usage to help the lovely natives. You can buy it online: it's called *Grammar and Punctuation for Key Stages 3 & 4, with Handy Usage Notes.* No, no, my opus isn't funny; it's a *proper* textbook. But it has lots of amusing examples of all sorts of grammatical, punctuation and usage errors which you see all around. Particularly in writing. And particularly if you are a foreigner in whom the importance of grammar was instilled from an early age.

Further on, I will enlarge on what else I did to become worthy of calling my adoptive country home, but this digression is becoming excessively long. Anyway, in light of the aforementioned, you shouldn't be surprised that I was crushed, absolutely crushed, to discover how I was perceived through the native eye.

> British passport – what a prize!
> It's your birthright, lucky guys,
> But, to aliens such as me,
> It's as precious as can be.

> So I greatly cherish mine,
> Notwithstanding its design:
> It's not just that it's not blue,
> But it clearly states 'EU'.

> Nothing's perfect; that aside,
> It does fill me with great pride,
> Which is why I often brag
> 'Bout my 'I am British' tag.

> Now, I lead a walking group;
> In that lovely, friendly troop
> There is Kian, nice enough,
> His demeanour somewhat bluff.

> Kian, hearing me thus boast,
> Looked as if he'd seen a ghost:
> "British passport? *You? How come?*"
> What a bummer – and then some:
>
> His appearance was so shocked
> That my world just shook and rocked;
> How much more toil, sweat and grit
> Till they see me as a Brit?

Admittedly, my accent is a huge impediment, it really is. For a long time, I have tried hard to affect native pronunciation. Oh, to speak like Sir Jacob Rees-Mogg! Surely, there would be few things left to desire then. Alas, alas… and I've suffered for it, I can tell you. One day, I approach the narrow suspension footbridge between Keswick and Portinscale, to which is affixed a large notice – in red – imploring cyclists to dismount. At both ends. I mean, the notice is affixed at both ends, which means that cyclists are also supposed to dismount at both ends. And I see a family of four riding on their bikes over the bridge and straight at me. Which means that they haven't dismounted. So, when the father draws level (I managed to squash myself against the railings), I respectfully point out the contents of the aforementioned notice. I mean, parents are supposed to set an example for their kids, aren't they? (The couple were accompanied by two children.) To which he glowers at me and angrily demands my name and address, commanding me to return to my *own* country forthwith because I 'shouldn't even be here'. Well, this happened after the Brexit vote, so perhaps I shouldn't have been so shocked. Wouldn't you want to protect your recently sovereign land from a foreign invasion?

But I've gone off at a tangent again, haven't I? Because, at the time of this chapter's mishap, I was still years away from joining any walking groups – let alone becoming a leader of one. And, of course, Britain was still oppressed by the EU. So anyway, this brilliant bus, X33, was pulled, alongside the so-called bike bus to Newby Bridge as well as several, albeit ephemeral, others servicing hard-to-reach areas – an absolute godsend to people like me. But they couldn't compete with the HS2. What a shame! Just when we were supposed to be saving the planet… While these buses were running, however, I made the fullest use of them, getting to far-flung places right across Cumbria. Judging by the reaction of my motorised friends, painstakingly acquired over subsequent years, I might as well have walked barefoot to the Gobi Desert.

But it's best to start at the beginning. In those early years, my exploration was limited to areas closer to Keswick. One of the buses I would use travelled to Buttermere over Honister Pass, the latter witnessing, over the next two-and-a-bit decades, numerous hopeful starts and weary endings, as well as a few inevitable frustrations when the return bus had been missed. The pass would later become my gateway to Pillar, Kirk Fell, Green and Great Gable, Fleetwith Pike, Haystacks & the Buttermere Ridge, Grey Knotts, Brandreth and even Base Brown.

On the other side of the pass rose Dale Head, which, I had decided, was going to be our first goal that morning. By our, I mean Vinnie's and mine. I had planned for us to climb it from the pass and then walk back all the way to Keswick over the ridge of High Spy, Maiden Moor and Catbells – a route which we had never attempted before but which looked very tempting on the map. A seasoned map reader, I hadn't yet acquired any guidebooks and didn't know any other walkers who might have been able to offer me handy tips.

We thus got off at the top of Honister Pass, where my eye was drawn to an inviting entrance to a comfortable-looking bridleway. Naturally, Vinnie and I followed it. The wide track veered left across the lower slopes of Dale Head, with hardly any incline: we were walking virtually on a level, though above a large field of scree tumbling right to the bottom of the valley. Were all Lakeland climbs *that* comfortable? Suddenly, we found ourselves facing an abrupt slope, and the track steepened considerably. Soon, we were scrambling up a narrow passage littered with loose slate and leading steeply up between two walls of darkly shadowed rock. The passage was intersected by horizontal platforms propped up by supports made of stones – clearly not structures erected with walkers in mind. They, in turn, were supporting what must once have been a miniature railway; we could still see some of its rusty metal remnants scattered about. It was obvious that we had earlier been lured onto an old quarry road and were now scrambling up towards a disused slate quarry, which we could see directly above, along the precarious route used by the miners from a bygone era to transport the quarried slate down to the pass. Drat! But one of my many annoying traits is my congenital propensity to plough on regardless. So Vinnie and I pressed unsteadily on, trying not to fall into any of the ominous looking quarry holes in the vicinity.

The higher we scrambled, the dicier the going got – nobody in their right mind would have chosen this route to climb to the summit of Dale Head. And nobody else did – certainly not on that day and probably not ever. When we finally scrambled to the top of the old works, suspended above the formidable rock face of Yew Crag, we caught a glimpse of a fence to our right. And, by the fence, something was moving. A human! We immediately made a beeline in that direction and could soon see a path running alongside the fence. What's more, there were other walkers following it – both below and above – and we knew that we had been granted salvation. Phew! This was the trail we should have been on all along – how did we manage to miss it? Or, rather, how did *I* contrive to miss it? For it was I who was behind all our mountain escapades, and, in fact, behind our move to the Lakes in the first place. I've always had this, slightly certifiable, streak. Though Vinnie might dispute this characterisation. No, not certifiable – slightly. Being a far more well-balanced human being than I could ever hope to be, he had sensibly decided that climbing mountains wasn't going to be his sole raison d'être, so it was I who would orchestrate each expedition, and the blunder was entirely on me. Not that he wasn't up to it. Far from it; he certainly had the body of a mountain conqueror.

He's fit and healthy (to my huge relief),
Looks great for his age and doesn't eat beef;
Such glorious physique
Is nigh-on unique;
Were I him, I'd remove this fig leaf.

Anyway, I have, since then, made countless ascents along this perfectly straightforward route, the entry to which is even properly signposted on the pass, so my error seems truly inexplicable. I would dearly love to say that it was a lesson learnt – but, alas, it wasn't (don't worry, there will be no more of 'of which laters').

The remainder of the climb was uneventful, the easy slope presenting no further obstacles. We paused on the summit to admire its splendid cairn, more akin to a column, before descending down the fell's steepish eastern slope, trying to dodge the scree as much as possible. Down below, nestling cosily in the hollow between Dale Head and High Spy, glistened Dalehead Tarn, and when we got to the water's edge, we enjoyed watching a little newt paddling energetically around with its little legs. The ascent of High Spy along its long southern ridge was relieved by awe-inspiring views of the formidable crags immediately to our left, whose brooding darkness sharply contrasted with the deep blueness of the sky above (is that sufficiently poetic for you?) An even more magnificent cairn awaited us on the summit. The comfortable descent to Maiden Moor, dominated by the fabulous vista of Skiddaw and Blencathra ahead, subsequently made an auspicious entry to my top ten best-ever ridge walks; it remains there to this day. From the barely discernible grassy top of Maiden Moor (has anybody ever managed to pinpoint it, Wainwright having failed in this endeavour?), one could clearly see lots of people on the neighbouring summit of Catbells, which, as we later discovered, was by far the most popular fell in the vicinity of Keswick – perhaps one best avoided in high season. Having ourselves made it to the crowded top, we executed a swift escape down the fell's attractive northern ridge, although we hadn't anticipated the few, thankfully quite easy, scrambles just below the summit.

In the course of the numerous climbs of Catbells we have made over the years, we witnessed the flip side of its popularity: people helplessly asking where the fell was or enquiring if we knew the way to the summit while standing right at the bottom of the obvious ridge route; people in flip-flops, high heels or similarly unsuitable footwear; people whose clothing wasn't even remotely appropriate for the occasion, or, indeed, with very little clothing on; even a lady determinedly trying to drag a pushchair containing an oblivious baby up the ridge. Mindful of the scrambles higher up, we presented her with a more realistic alternative. Thankfully, we were sufficiently persuasive on this particular occasion.

Some mothers do have them… then again, maybe I wasn't much better. After all, what sane person would have dragged an unsuspecting companion up a steep, exposed and highly unstable slope pockmarked with dangerous holes? Just as well that my lawfully wedded isn't easily flustered.

> When I panic, dash and fret,
> Husband doesn't break a sweat,
> Neither does he give a frown,
> Simply saying, "Just calm down,"
> For he's always, as a rule,
> Mr Calm and Mr Cool.

Deadline looms, what wretched fix!
Husband's eyelid never flicks;
As I'm stressing to the max,
Husband calmly says, "Relax,"
For he's always, as a rule,
Mr Calm and Mr Cool.

Never wanting to be late,
I leave early – and then wait;
Husband's never in a flush:
"Take it easy; what's the rush?"
For he's always, as a rule,
Mr Calm and Mr Cool.

And when time for him runs out,
He will, without any doubt,
Say, with not a hint of sorrow,
"I won't go until tomorrow,"
For he's always, as a rule,
Mr Calm and Mr Cool!

Thankfully, time didn't run out for him on this particular occasion – or, indeed, on any other after that – although he might have come close on the precipitous crags high above Shamrock Traverse on Pillar, which we later (no, not on the same day) climbed from Buttermere. But that's another story entirely.

6

Cumbrian Buses and the Mardale Head Blunder

They say that Britain – particularly its western counties – has only two seasons: the wet one and the very wet one. I don't think it's strictly true, although, admittedly, British weather is nothing like that in Poland, which used to have four properly delineated seasons, each in its correctly designated slot. But Britain also has four. It's just that they can all occur in one day – if not in one hour.

> I am neither glum nor sour:
> Polish weather could be dour –
> *Fickle* it was *not*;
> *Here*, the picture's fraught:
> *Four* seasons there are in *one* hour.

Our local bus provider, Stagecoach, adopts a different classification, diving the year into two seasons: the winter one and the summer one. It then publishes two timetables:

one for winter and one for summer, the former, entirely understandably, offering fewer services than the latter. Throughout winter, I am thus on an anxious countdown. Swallows as a harbinger of spring? Forget it: for me, spring comes when the first Buttermere bus appears.

But there is more: the summer season is a bit like a Russian, or matryoshka, doll, containing within it the high season, when schools break up for the summer. It's then that a wave of humanity washes up on the shores of Derwentwater and our other lakes, blocking roads to all beauty spots with crazily parked vehicles and leaving in its wake discarded camping equipment and barbecues, cans of nitrous oxide, laughing gas canisters, condoms (I hope no children are reading this book), broken bottles, leftover food, toilet waste and all manner of other human detritus. I mean when lots of lovely tourists, determined to support the local economy as much as they can and appropriately kitted out, visit our enchanting county with every intention of respecting the countryside code to the letter while exploring the area by public transport or by bike or, indeed, on foot.

So, in high season, albeit on Sundays only, we used to get these small buses facilitating incursions into remote corners of the Lake District. I have already mentioned the Mardale Head bus, haven't I? Mardale Head sits at the south-western tip of Haweswater Reservoir, offering access to several magnificent fells looming right above, whose dramatic crags tumble down to the valley bottom in a most eye-catching fashion.

Admittedly, the bus in question started not from Keswick but from Penrith, so one first needed to catch an early bus to get oneself there. But I was used to early starts: in the Polish Tatras, I would regularly get up before 5am so that I could travel on the first bus of the day. My certifiability had, clearly, taken hold when I was still in my teens.

Meanwhile in Keswick: five weeks, four weeks, three weeks, two weeks, one week – yippee, the Mardale Head bus was about to start running! By then, I had acquired the seven Wainwright guides and realised that I had done so much climbing that scaling the remaining Lakeland fells was well within my grasp. But how to reach that remote rest? That's where the Mardale Head bus came in.

I needed to climb Grey Crag and Tarn Crag, sitting on the far eastern fringes of Lakeland above Longsleddale. Facing some fifteen miles and three separate ascents, I needed to start early. But, before I get going with the tale, I can't resist a little boast (my boasts are always modest in size – you'll see). You will have undoubtedly noticed that I have used miles rather than kilometres (and, when earlier imprisoned in the lift, I panicked in imperial measures). Impressive or what? We in Europe – not that Britain is not in Europe, but with all the stuff going on recently, one might be excused for forming the impression that it has relocated to a different hemisphere lock, stock and barrel – anyway, we in Europe grew up with the metric system. You will thus indubitably conclude that my declaration, made in the previous chapter, to have made strenuous efforts to assimilate, integrate and blend was not merely empty rhetoric. So when the greatest benefit of Brexit, namely the expungement of all metric measures, comes to pass, I will be laughing, won't I? I have written the ditty below to cheer up Sir Jacob Rees-Mogg, the architect of this inspired scheme, in case he is a little upset to have been returned to the back benches after a brief period of glory in Liz Truss's cabinet. But at least he's got his knighthood now; I'm sure it's richly deserved. After all, the honour was bestowed on him by Boris Johnson, himself a paragon of good judgement, honesty and moral rectitude.

> They are our country's treasures,
> These good old imperial measures:
> There's an inch, a foot, a mile,
> We all use them; that's our style.
>
> There is, near a local mine,
> A peculiar-looking sign,
> It says it's '2m' to Grange;
> Underneath, there's something strange:
>
> It points to a car park which
> Is no more than just a pitch
> But which isn't very far,
> Its sign, though, is most bizarre:
>
> It says – look, it's '100m'!
> Now, this is a real gem:
> Who would drive one hundred miles
> Just to park? (I like your smiles.)
>
> But it's *metres* – see my point?
> Such confusions disappoint
> But are common nowadays:
> Let's revert to good old ways!

> Who would say (not even Peter),
> "I won't give a centimetre!"
> And a gallon or an ounce
> Only traitors would renounce;
>
> They are common, trusted, sound –
> And don't start me on the pound!
> Rees-Mogg, thus, with all his clout,
> Will ensure it's sorted out.
>
> I am sure you get my drift:
> This is Brexit's greatest gift,
> Whose importance is material –
> We're reverting to imperial!
>
> Hallelujah!

Anyway, I needed an early start, so Mardale Head would be no good: the earliest I could get there would be far too late for the enterprise to stand any chance of succeeding. A-a-a, but I could *finish* there! So I hopped on an early bus to Ings (sitting by the A591 between Windermere and Kendal), whence (not *from* whence) I struck out for Kentmere. The undulating bridleway, starting at the pleasantly elevated hamlet of Grassgarth above Ings, was wide and comfortable, and I made good progress, although the leaden sky hung low, looking menacing. But, as I might have mentioned once or twice (or, possibly, three times), not only did my return bus run once a week only, but it was limited to the short high season, and I simply couldn't afford to waste a whole week. As the lovely natives perceptively observe, beggars can't be choosers.

After four-plus miles, I descended to Kentmere right opposite the magnificent Kentmere Hall, whose ancient-looking tower had apparently been constructed in 1320. Wow! But there was no time to stop and stare because I had to climb out of the village, cosily ensconced in the secluded valley at the mouth of the iconic Kentmere Horseshoe. With thick mist swathing all the tops, I couldn't appreciate the horseshoe's magnificence, but I hadn't come there to admire the views, had I? After ascending to the pass between the sprawling Green Quarter Fell (described in Wainwright's *Outlying Fells*) and Shipman Knotts, the first (or last) fell in the horseshoe, I went down to the remote Sadgill, which sits at the terminus of the minor and very lengthy road running along the bottom of Longsleddale. Not for nothing is the valley called long. Sadgill is where normal people would start their conquest of both fells, but it took me eight miles just to get there. Perhaps I should have persevered with my driving lessons, after all. Then again, Dom would have probably needed to buy up the entire local supply of Valerian.

By now, the foreboding sky had fulfilled its threat, producing a rather unpleasant drizzle. Stubbornly ignoring Wainwright's sage advice to leave Grey Crag alone in mist, I stood at the bottom of a steep grassy slope crowned with a bulwark of rocks. Where the hell was this path? Neither summit was visible, and I grimly decided that I had no choice but to start climbing blind. How, after exercising similar judgement for the past quarter of a century, I am still with you, I will never fathom. Thankfully, by the time I got to the first wall I spied a narrow trail and followed it up along a steep gully clad in burgeoning bracken, whose wet branches enveloped me with every step, finishing the job started by the drizzle. With limited visibility, I stuck to the path like glue, eventually emerging on the summit of Grey Crag – though not before several unintended deviations. Thankfully, the cloud dispersed a little, and I caught a glimpse of the slightly higher top of the neighbouring Tarn Crag, adorned with a large survey post. By Jove, Wainwright had been right: the summit of Grey Crag barely rose above the vast plateau of which the fell was a part, which would make navigation hopeless if there was no visibility.

And, although I always carried a map, I had never learnt how to use a compass. Or an app. I don't like apps anyway; apparently, they can infect you with a virus. But, in those days, I didn't even have a mobile phone. After all, I had survived countless adventures in the Polish Tatras without one, so what was all the fuss about? At this juncture, it might be an idea to paint you a picture of my map-reading prowess – albeit in the third person. In similar circumstances, it's always best to distance oneself from the subject a little.

> "Map reading is *never* a test."
> She speaks as if she were the best:
> She won't use an app,
> Just looks at her map,
> Then aims east but, alas, ends up west.

Well, not always. But, if (heaven forfend) this book should ever fall into the hands of your offspring (perhaps you could lock it up or something), I suggest you impress on them the imperative not to follow my example.

Anyway, the guidebook – thankfully – now sent me towards the fence, suggesting that this was the best way of avoiding the marshes of Greycrag Tarn. While, to this day, I haven't tested the soundness of this advice, the recommended passage between the two fells rather strained my endurance: if you want to enjoy the walk, don't attempt it in anything other than prolonged dry conditions – if such a rarity should occur. Well, I'm probably laying it on a bit thick here: after all, I subsequently climbed both fells another eight times, but you get my drift. Another fence guided me from Tarn Crag down towards horrid moss hags just above the bottom of Mosedale. But, to be honest, I was so wet and muddy that I was past caring. In my discomfort, I tried to distract myself by composing this limerick.

> Wishing this were just a blip,
> All you hear is drip, drip, drip;
> In this pouring rain,
> You are soaked again
> Right from your top to your tip.

Surprisingly, it didn't appear to help very much, so I decided that I needed to compare my predicament with something truly awful – far worse than my plight. Suddenly, I slipped on a wet stone and fell, getting even wetter than I was already. And more muddy. I sat on a rock to compose myself, and then it came to me: Beast from the East! I certainly wasn't nearly as badly off as those caught up in it back in 2018. And if I could finish my creation on a positive note to cheer myself up…

> We were blasted by the Beast,
> Blown straight over from the East;
> Fed by northern polar vortex,
> It would slice right through your cortex,
> Landing an almighty blow
> With its gales and frost and snow,
> Blizzards, whiteouts, drifts and ice;
> And there was, indeed, a price
> If you tried to brave this storm:
> You could *not* stay dry or warm.
>
> So to end up safe and sound,
> You wrapped up and went to ground,
> Keeping all essentials handy,
> Namely whiskey, rum and brandy;
> Soon, your innards were ablaze,
> With you swaying in a haze,
> Feeling comfy, snug and cosy,
> Both your cheeks and nose quite rosy;
> This is how (you get my drift?)
> Best to deal with Putin's 'gift'.

Propelled by the alluring vision of warmth and cosiness, I got up and continued further down to the bottom of Longsleddale. There I stood and trembled: high above me was the top of Gatescarth Pass, which I needed to climb over to get to Mardale Head with its prospect of salvation – there was no other way. The bridleway may have been comfortable, but, at this stage in the proceedings, I was barely dragging my feet, cold, wet and tired. What I haven't told you yet is that, in those early days, I hadn't discovered Páramo. If I had been wearing its excellent clothing, I might have fared better, but I wasn't.

> Páramo's a famous brand;
> If you've got a ramble planned,
> Get yourself some decent gear;
> Thankfully, my shop is near,
> And I visit every week,
> For I can't resist a peek;
> But a peek is not enough:
> I keep buying all the stuff!

No, I'm not on commission, but, if I tell them that I have mentioned them in this book, they may all go and buy it. Just as I buy loads from them. *Loads*. So come on, guys, you can stretch to a few measly quid.

Anyway, I did perk up on the top of the pass: no more climbing! Time, however, was now running out. I was, after all, on a schedule: the bus wasn't going to know that I was descending in its direction and wait for me. So I put on as much speed as I could muster and reached my destination just in time for the last bus. Only – there was *no* bus! No, no, I wasn't late: the bus simply hadn't started running that season *at all*. Bummer! I had misread the timetable, failing to realise that it would be the on the *following* Sunday, not *this* one, that the bus would start. So there I was, by myself, far from civilisation and without any means of escape. And with no mobile phone even. Thankfully, Mardale

Head is popular with tourists, and even on a miserable day you are likely to come across some hardy, or should it be foolhardy, souls, two of whom took pity on me and offered me a lift to Penrith.

There, I stood in the bus station toilet by the hand-drier, which, on this occasion, became a leg-drier: I would pull each knee towards my chin as high as I could, exposing it to the blast of hot air. Wonderful! Slightly drier, I spent the long wait for the Keswick bus (in those days, Sunday buses between the two towns ran only every two hours, so there has been *some* improvement since then: these days, they run every hour), reviving myself with some refreshments at a local hotel and killing time by composing these silly ditties.

A Good Question

At the gates of Hell,
"You'll have woes!" they yell,
While, at Heaven's door,
"You'll have peace," they swore;
Neither is the one:
"Where will I have fun?"

Alarmed

"This door is alarmed." "By what? Something major?"
"By people like you, it's quite safe to wager."

On my late return home, I asked Vinnie if he had been worried. He gave me a resigned look and shook his head.

"I know what you are like; you with your mad escapades."

At that point, I'd already had several years' worth of Lakeland exploration under my belt, most of it undertaken by myself. I think I've already explained that Vinnie is a well-rounded human being with better things to do than climbing mountains day in, day out.

To this day, I haven't decided which the preferable way of missing the return bus is: being too late or too early for it. But I haven't yet told you about my in-depth experience of the former. I think an apposite example should follow next, don't you?

7

Culture Clashes, the Green Crag Lunacy and Human Insatiability

In my first, single-minded, quest to bag all 214 Wainwright fells, I had now picked all the low-hanging fruit. *Low-hanging-fruit* – ha! Aren't you impressed by my linguistic flourish? It has taken me a long time to finesse it, you know. But, hey, I had worked in British offices for many years, prominent, or should I say foremost, among them being the Foremost Authority for the Regulation of Transformation (FART for short). OK, so I've made this name up; otherwise, I might have been sued by my former employer. But the office did exist; ask my therapist. I needed twenty one-hour sessions to get over the experience. And she wasn't cheap, I can tell you.

You won't believe the colloquialisms I picked up at FART. And idioms. And all sorts of other interesting stuff. No, not English grammar: the one I had smuggled into Britain with me was pretty sound, even if some of it baffled my native-born colleagues. For example, quite a few didn't have a clue

– *not a clue* – about dangling participles. Dangling *what*? Actually, this grammatical error can be so funny that I have written a whole book about it. It's called *Hilarity with Misrelated Participles*. Or discontinuous modification – what's this when it's at home? And when I mentioned all manner of other misrelated constructions, their eyes would just glaze over. Greengrocer's apostrophe seemed to perplex quite a few. One colleague even asked if it was tasty, his palate being on the refined side. And don't even get me started on the comma splice. You just plonk the comma wherever you like, don't you? And do we need it at all? Let's face it, it's just a blooming nuisance most of the time. No idea that punctuation is largely governed by grammar – *no idea at all*. That's what happens when a country thinks that the study of grammar stifles creativity. And Britain set great store by creativity. Thankfully, this wonderful country did wake up in the noughties, but several decades of neglect left their mark, providing me with an abundance of examples of mangled grammar, crazy punctuation and mutilated usage, many of them unintentionally hilarious, for my books and articles.

Back in the offices of FART, my colleagues' vocabulary was amazing, absolutely amazing! Before, however, I reached their dizzying standard, there had been a few cultural clashes and linguistic misunderstandings along the way, I won't lie. I'm sure that the ones below will suffice to illustrate the considerable barriers I had to overcome.

"Step up to the plate," they say,
"You mean *climb*?" (My sheer dismay!)
"I've arranged the plates myself:
They are on the *bottom* shelf."

"Think outside the box," they add,
And this makes me rather glad:
Boxes may be fine for pets,
But, inside, a human sweats.

"We must benchmark," they then state,
This is, though, one thing I hate;
"Marking benches," I thus shout,
"Is for vandals – count me out!"

Drilling down, throughout the place,
They are able to touch base;
So I say, "Guys, you are brill,
You must have a sturdy drill."

Hitting the ground running does
Seem to set them all abuzz,
But it must be painful, so
I do caution, "Do be slow."

Forward planning is their cry,
It's so silly I just sigh:
"When did you plan *backwards* last?"
To which they all look aghast.

And their feedback loop (I grieve)
Is so often negative;
"Guys, this smacks of sheer defeat –
Look at BoJo: he's upbeat!"

Our road map must, just must,
Be grand, solid and robust;
My reaction's quite elated:
"All my maps are laminated!"

Picking the low-hanging fruit
Is a move that seems astute:
"My allotment is close by,
Let's pick apples and make pie."

For some reason, all those guys
Have been curt with their replies,
Giving me a hostile glare,
And I found this hard to bear.

Oops, I may be in danger of exceeding my allowance of digressions and asides (if you will pardon the tautology) here, so I'd better return to my mountain escapades – sharpish. Green Crag certainly wasn't hanging low, that's for sure. It was (and still is, actually) tucked far away, clinging to the southernmost edge of Lakeland above Eskdale, my favourite valley by a mile. I have wondered whether my ardour is being fuelled by the dale's inaccessibility to the likes of me: things which are hard to get are often tempting to a degree not necessarily commensurate with their actual worth. But surely not Eskdale.

Actually, Green Crag had been quite lucky to have made it into the Wainwright guide on the Southern Lakes at all, being surrounded by sprawling outliers stretching out to the Irish Sea. In order to finish climbing all the Wainwright fells, I needed to get to it. A small question remained: how exactly? I did mention our touristy summer buses, which, coupled with a degree of luck, offered me a solution, but not even the highest of seasons would have induced our esteemed bus operator to lay on a service to such a remote area. After all, with everyone firmly wedded to their cars, their clientele would have been insufficient to justify the bother. This is a capitalist country, so no dosh – no dice.

The route I had contrived looked doable on the map. Lucky that, in those early days, I wasn't checking the distance in advance of any walk. If I had, I would have discovered that it was some twenty-one miles – not quite a marathon but with plenty of ascent to make up for the deficiency. But I was still in my immortal phase – although only just.

The sun had barely risen when I dashed across our ghost-like town to the bus station to catch a very early bus to Seatoller in Borrowdale – my local valley. In those days, our buses used to start much earlier than today, carrying one or two nodding hospitality workers – and me. I wonder if they ever marvelled at the sheer insanity of getting up that early without being compelled to do so. But I *did* feel compelled.

Motorists always drive all the way to Seathwaite, a farm tucked away in a very picturesque corner of Borrowdale, surrounded by magnificent mountains (both the valley and the farm). The place has the dubious distinction of being the wettest inhabited locality in the United (or should it now be Disunited) Kingdom. I, of course, had to walk along the road from the bus stop at Seatoller, but what's a mile-and-a-bit when you are rested and raring to go? Ascending along Grains Gill to Esk Hause – at nearly 2,500 feet, one of the highest mountain passes in the Lake District – I amused myself by playing my little game: is it still going to be two hours and five minutes to the top of the pass? It was! (It wouldn't be now.) I had trodden, and timed, the route numerous times, always awe-struck by the towering north face of Great End ahead, riven by formidable gullies, where many an adventurer had come a cropper. Thankfully, I was never *that* insane, though I had come close.

What I hadn't done before was descend from Esk Hause, a busy high-level thoroughfare attracting crowds bound for Scafell Pike, to Upper Eskdale, which stretched out for miles at my feet. A ravine between steep craggy slopes of Esk Pike on one side and Ill Crag on the other and filled with loose rocks and scree conveyed me down to the bottom of the eerily deserted valley. Well, it would be, wouldn't it? It was miles away from civilisation. I meandered along the widening dale, enclosed by vertiginous rocks of Scafell Pike, Scafell and Slight Side (nothing slight about it, I promise), soaring high into the sky to the west, and the long shoulders of the lower (but by no means low) Esk Pike and Hard Knott to the east. Delighting in the shapely pyramid of Harter Fell ahead, I finally reached Hardknott Road, running along the length of Eskdale, which, at this point, was no longer Upper. Strictly speaking, that's where my hike should have begun, but I'd already covered ten miles. Not that I particularly felt it: the magnetic pull of an unclimbed fell was too strong for any weariness to set in. So I quickly crossed the road and started my climb of Green Crag, my excitement mounting with every step. The rocky summit rose above the sprawling upland expanse of Birker Fell, which stretched out for miles and miles. I surveyed the unfamiliar area with a profound sense of satisfaction: I have finally bagged my fell!

But it was a *long* way away from the bus. Suddenly aware of the distance already travelled, I trudged across the wet grassy depression between my mountain and Harter Fell, which seemed interminable (the depression – not Harter Fell, which looks appealing from all directions). The partially wooded descent to the bottom of the Duddon Valley was far more attractive, and the remote, now vibrantly verdant, vale itself an utter delight – even to an already tired wayfarer. What now? Actually, I *did* know what now: an ascent up a mountain pass called Walna Scar in the Coniston Fells. But I was right at the bottom of the valley, and the Walna Scar Pass, at 2,000 feet, was high up. And it was my only escape route. Somehow, I made it to the top of the pass, although it was on my hands and knees that I finally reached it. From there, I could at last see faint signs of civilisation in the distance. Too tired to rejoice, I plodded down towards Coniston in the falling dusk, not even bothering to check the watch: by the time I made it to the village, the last bus would be certain to have already gone.

By then, however, I had made progress in one important respect: in the face of the unstoppable march of modernity, I had caved in and acquired a mobile phone. Nothing fancy – not one of these all-singing, all-dancing contraptions – just an ordinary dumbphone. (Actually, I use one to this day, dinosaur that I am.) My phone may have been dumb, but it made calls, and that's all I asked of it. So I called Garry with the taxicab. He was my rescuer on many of those occasions when I had missed the last bus home. As we travelled, we chatted, and, in the end, I felt that we had got to know each other pretty well. It was thus Garry to whom I turned when I needed help with the publishing of one of my books. In case you were wondering why, I must tell you about my experience of dealing with British literary agents and book publishers, which is long, colourful and exasperating. If you don't know much about the travails involved in trying to get a book published, and maybe even need a little advice, here is what to brace yourself for.

> All of them are godlike creatures
> Seeking quite groundbreaking features –
> All those folk who publish books:
> It's much harder than it looks,
>
> So for impact one must brace,
> And one's book must be plain ace;
> One thus polishes and tinkers,
> Trying hard to shed one's blinkers,
>
> Then, at long last, the book's ready:
> It's a feeling that is heady,
> But one must, and without fail,
> Go pursue the holy grail:
>
> Oh, to see the book in print
> And, perhaps, to make a mint!
> Now, what do those deities want?
> First of all, it's Arial font,

Fifty pages. Spacing? Double,
A synopsis – that's no trouble,
But make sure it's just one page;
Otherwise, they'll disengage.

Now, the letter, and that's it:
You are ready to submit!
Then you notice (you've been slow):
'Agents only' – what a blow!

Agents are quite godlike, too:
They'll be wanting something new;
What is it that they demand?
Times New Roman will be grand.

Spacing? One line and a half,
Then they want a paragraph
Which is paramount and which
Is your elevator pitch.

A synopsis has to be
Rather longer; your CV
Must, of course, be tailor-made,
Or you'll never make the grade.

It's three chapters they are after;
Though you are a good re-drafter,
You express yourself in verse –
It has gone from bad to worse;

Then you see (to top it all)
A decree that makes you bawl:
"We'll consider your creation –
After a recommendation."

But who from? To whom to turn?
You can't hide your great concern.
It transpires they prefer
Someone who's a connoisseur,

But you work in solitude:
You feel well and truly screwed,
Mercifully, you then find
Someone who's a mastermind

In your local pub-quiz team;
They might help you with your scheme.
You enquire, your heart racing,
"Are you happy with my spacing?"

"Spacing? Why? It's all the same;
What's at stake is my good name."
"But I cannot understand:
I just want a helping hand."

"This is what they *all* would say,
But I might just rue the day;
Now, imagine this scenario:
Not unlike an impresario,

"I do offer you my backing,
But the Agent finds you lacking!
It would not be very nice;
Listen to this sage advice:

"You *must* find a man who would
Come to me and vouch you're good."
You're distraught but say, "I see,
"So who might this person be?"

"I would like a weighty beast:
A policeman or a priest."
"I know neither but could nab
Garry with the taxicab…"

And so, on and on it goes,
Which, quite evidently, shows
How this, most amazing, nation
Values a recommendation.

So, if you should ever fancy having your book published, you'd better rustle up some recommenders. Whatever you do, though, stay away from Garry – he's mine. His phone number had become indelibly imprinted on my memory after one too many strandings in the middle of nowhere. Hardly had there been a more consequential thing to memorise, I can tell you. Collapsed on some village bench after my Green Crag escapade, I was finally rescued by him, albeit after nearly an hour's wait, and delivered home, where Vinnie greeted me with his, by now customary, headshake. Thankfully, he had been fed by my lovely mum (may she rest in peace), who used to spoil us rotten by cooking all our dinners. Admittedly, mine was in the bin by then, but, past caring, all I wanted was bed. And Vinnie greatly benefitted from this arrangement, anyway. No, there was no arrangement to customarily chuck my dinners in the bin; I mean our being fed by my mum: a domestic goddess I certainly am not, being severely deficient in the culinary department (as well as in many others, but this book is supposed to entertain – *not* depress – you).

That, however, wasn't the end of it: I still had other hard-to-reach fells to climb before I could stake a claim to having bagged all 214 Wainwright fells. Which, as you already know, I subsequently did, so there will be more tales there. And, while most (all?) sane people would consider scaling all Lakeland mountains once as quite sufficient to satisfy their esteem needs (sitting at level four in Maslow's hierarchy of needs), I'm not endowed with similar rationality. So, as I've also told you, I kept on going until I climbed every single Lakeland fell at least nine times; in fact, I have nearly completed all my tenth climbs. But I'm definitely stopping at ten – *definitely!* Then again…

> I know I'd be rapt, my life would be zen,
> If only I could slim down to size ten,
> I sweat as I try – my efforts are great –
> And now that I'm there, I'd like to be eight…
>
> If only I got a salary hike:
> At least fifty grand is what I would like;
> They gave me (wait!) sixty: yippee, this is brill!
> But then, sixty-five would feel better still…

If only I could win fortune and fame,
I would be so thrilled they all knew my name;
And now that I have, they're all after me:
I wish that I were a no-one and free…

If only this verse could win the first prize,
I'd want nothing else, I promise you, guys;
My wish just came true, I'd prayed that it would;
Now please judge the rest and tell me they're good…

If only I could climb all Lakeland tops –
This day would be when my quest, *surely*, stops;
And it has arrived: I've just scaled my last!
I'm starting again; no, don't look aghast.

If only I could stop pining for more,
Stop finding new things to crave and ask for,
My life as it is might just be my dish;
Of course, I could do – just one final wish?

The insatiability of the human appetite!

8

Human Memory, the World King and My Harter Fell Escapade

Human appetite may be limitless, but human memory is definitely short. Mine is, anyway. Why else would I even countenance undertaking an expedition which had every chance of turning into something similar to my Green Crag odyssey? And so soon, at that? But Harter Fell still remained unclimbed. So it had to be conquered. Harter Fell is, however, a next-door neighbour of Green Crag, which means that it's remote and hard to reach, occupying a prime position between Eskdale and the Duddon Valley. And to reach the Duddon Valley, I needed to get myself to Coniston and then walk over the Walna Scar Pass again before I could home in on my next objective from the bottom of the valley, which is where a motorised person would start from. And then, after descending from the summit of Harter Fell, I would have to scale another fell, Hard Knott, and execute my third descent of the day before climbing even higher and going down yet again so that I could finally reach my saviour bus in Great Langdale. But, as I've said, human memory is short.

Take politicians. They promise you the earth, but you have already forgotten that they promised you the earth the last time, so you vote for them again. And then what happens? Remember when Boris Johnson was on his single-minded quest to become World King? I mean our Prime Minister. We were assured, *categorically assured*, by both him and other politicians that, as soon as we freed ourselves from the bondage imposed on us by the imperialist EU, we would reach all these sunlit uplands and attain world dominance, so when can we expect them, please? But, back then, it was easy to get caught up in all the frenzied excitement, with the prospect of Britain finally regaining her freedom and, at long last, being able to trade with Tonga on the horizon (no, Tonga was too far to be on the horizon; I meant the prospect. One can have tremendous fun with unintentionally hilarious word order). Remember: global Britain and all that? Oh, those heady days, full of tantalising promise! Actually, I thought I had got the measure of Johnson rather early, when he was a mere foreign secretary in the government headed by Theresa May. So struck was I by his Churchillian greatness that I felt compelled to pay him a little homage. This one goes back to 2018.

> I am a one-nation Tory
> Who cares not a jot for glory,
> Am your quintessential Brit
> Appreciated for my wit
> And a slightly raffish look;

I know how to write a book
And draw lots of nice red lines,
Am a connoisseur of wines,
And I never, ever never tire
When suspended from zip wire.

When our greatness is at stake,
I will (always) have my cake
And will eat it – hence my girth
(Please contain unseemly mirth);
Round the world I widely roam
(Though I never take a comb),
And I think you ought to ditch
Your displeasure with the rich;
In a nutshell, that is that;
Let me tell you where we're at

Vis-à-vis our negotiation
Re the freedom of our nation.
I'd kept strictly off Grand Marnier,
When I told this old chap Barnier
He could go and jolly whistle;
Fair enough: he didn't bristle
But came out with poppycock
'Bout the ticking of the clock;
We are *not*, so as you know,
Giving Barnier any dough;

Of this there can be no doubt:
After all, we're getting out;
Trust me: you can go and chill.

> *What?* We're paying *20 bill?*
> Nah, not on your blinking nelly!
> (I'll repeat this on the telly),
> Not if I can… wait a sec,
> PM's waving a fat cheque…
> It says 40 – but that's *double!*
> Grrrr, we really are in trouble:
>
> That's the dosh, I acquiesce,
> Promised to the NHS;
> Payout wasn't in our plan –
> Things are going down the pan;
> But fear not (I'm being frank):
> With a tiger in my tank,
> I will cut us such a deal
> It will strike you as a steal;
> I just need a single thing:
> Coronation as World King!

So we duly crowned him. I mean elected his as our prime minister.

Goodness me, how on earth did I manage to stray so far from Harter Fell? I think I had started telling you about the planning of my conquest thereof while, clearly, overcome by amnesia. Having drawn up a plan of action, I booked Garry with the taxicab for first thing in the morning because I needed to get to Ambleside in time for an early bus to Coniston. So far, so good. I was, by then, well acquainted with the bridleway leading from Coniston up to Walna Scar because you had to use it as a gateway to the Old Man of Coniston, one of the iconic Lakeland mountains. From the top of the pass, Harter Fell, preening itself straight ahead, looked magnificent, commanding the Duddon Valley with an easy assurance clearly emanating from the consciousness of its unsurpassed beauty. It was barely higher than the pass I stood on. What a shame that I had to go all the way down to the bottom of the valley before I could reach its summit.

And do you know what? I had always been opposed to turning the Lake District into a theme park, but, at that point, it crossed my mind that if someone would just run a zip wire, or perhaps even a gondola, between the pass at the summit, I could just zoom straight across. Wouldn't that be nice? No, no, perish the thought: I'm ruining my credentials here. Actually, have I established any credentials to speak of in this book? I'm beginning to worry…

Anyway, down and down I go, right to the valley bottom, as before vibrantly verdant, before crossing the River Duddon over these huge stepping stones (even marked on the *Ordnance Survey* map). Before you get too impressed, though, I am an awful water crosser, always terrified of slipping off a wet stone and falling into the water, and would have never attempted the crossing if they hadn't had this solid metal wire (actually, a wire is always supposed to be metal) running above the line of the stones from one side of the river to the other. But they had, and the crossing was quite fun. A delightful bridleway passing by Grassguards in the Dunnerdale Forest conveyed me upwards to the edge of the open plateau of Ulpha Fell, from where I could complete my climb. Another Wainwright scaled! And what a beautiful summit, adorned with three rocky tors (at times, it's not easy to avoid tautology: tors are meant to be rocky), forming an attractive craggy cluster, just about climbable by the likes of me. Wainwright was right: the descent to Hardknott Pass was swampy and not particularly appealing, although the tedium was relieved by an impressive view of the precipitous rocky wall of Raven Crag, determinedly defending the southern flank of Hard Knott and rising steeply from the pass.

In theory, I could have tried to scrounge a lift off some daring motorist braving the steep and winding road leading over the pass (my friend Clive calls similar roads a corkscrew), but I tend not to do this. After all, aren't I supposed to be an advocate of carless exploration of the Lake District? So all I did was cast a furtive, albeit desirous, glance at the passing car and commenced my muddy ascent of Hard Knott. While nowhere near as attractive as its neighbour, the fell offers an amazing view of several Lakeland giants, from Slight Side through Scafell, Scafell Pike, Ill Crag, Esk Pike and Bowfell to Crinkle Crags, all sharply delineated against the azure sky and, on that clear day, appearing to be within touching distance. (You didn't think I would be stupid enough to attempt a walk such as this in poor visibility, did you? Then again, this mishap on Skiddaw, when I needed the mountain rescue… but that's another story entirely, which will follow shortly.)

Hard Knott wasn't new to me despite its remote setting. I bet you are wondering how I had managed to reach it earlier. Your curiosity is about to be satisfied: a bus to Ambleside, another bus to the New Dungeon Ghyll Hotel in Great Langdale, up along The Band to the high pass between Bow Fell and Crinkle Crags called Three

Tarns, down all the way to the bottom of Moasdale (or Mosedale), up the long northern shoulder of Hard Knott to the summit, down the long northern shoulder of Hard Knott all the way back to the bottom of Moasdale, up to the Three Tarns again and then back down The Band to the New Dungeon Ghyll, with the usual denouement of getting stranded in Great Langdale after the last bus has left. At least it was only twelve miles (six each way), but you had three separate climbs (two to the high pass and one up Hard Knott). And, in those days, Great Langdale definitely had a problem.

> You can have a brilliant scramble
> When you do a Langdale ramble:
> First, you have a lovely ride
> All the way to Ambleside,
> Then you change for Dungeon Ghyll,
> Waiting keenly for the thrill
> Of Bow Fell and Crinkle Crags
> And forgetting all the snags
> Which bus users' days can mar
> In this land in thrall to car.
>
> Then you claim your glorious booty
> Amid fells of splendid beauty,
> Where you'd roam all day, but no:
> You've a bus to catch – you go;
> And though you would rather walk,
> You must really beat the clock,
> So you run and sweat and stumble,
> Trying, vainly, not to grumble

> 'Cos your bus, I kid you not,
> Leaves at four – a right tight spot!

Admittedly, things have improved since then, with the last bus now leaving later, but, on the day of my Harter Fell adventure, this improvement was still years away. Which is why Great Langdale had borne witness to my sprints of such velocity that I could easily have given Usain Bolt a run for his money. When, however, trying to return from there after climbing Hard Knott in the way described above, even a one-minute mile would have got me nowhere.

Anyway, I haven't finished my Harter Fell story yet. But, as you know, I was already on the summit of Hard Knott, so you have probably guessed how I managed to extricate myself. Yep, by heading to Great Langdale over the high pass. And, naturally, I missed the last bus from there, so it had to be a taxi to Ambleside, from where, mercifully, the last bus to Keswick was yet to depart.

Hold on a moment, do you know what I've just realised? This book was supposed to paint you a seductive picture of all those lovely Lakeland walks which could be enjoyed without the recourse to a car, but it seems to be heading in the opposite direction. Bummer!

9

The Three-Valley Marathon, Nuts and Bus Drivers

No, it is unpardonable, it really is. I mean my (*not* me) painting such an unflattering picture of the public transport in the Lakes. What was I thinking of? After all, our lovely buses have carried me the length and breadth of our delightful county, enabling me to climb all the fells therein (and even some thereout) many times over. It is thus high time I put forth a counter-claim. But first, I need to set the scene.

If you want to do a Wasdale walk, you start at Wasdale. If you want to do an Ennerdale walk, you start at Ennerdale. No sane person would attempt *both walks together* while starting from Borrowdale. But, if memory serves me right, I haven't staked any claims to sanity here, have I? After all, not for nothing does the book contain 'lunacies' in its title. So I order a taxi for 6am and tell my lawfully wedded that we are off for a nice walk. "Fine," says he, being all in favour of nice walks. Actually, I would have ordered our carriage for earlier because, unlike Vinnie, I knew what lay in store, but they charged double before 6am, and we weren't made of money. By 'they' I mean our friendly local taxi firm, Garry having opted to have a lie-in that morning.

So we hop in and get a delightful ride to Seathwaite, the charming hamlet being ensconced deep in the bowels of Borrowdale. I've already told you about Seathwaite's unenviable precipitation record, haven't I? But, for this particular walk, we needed the weather's cooperation, which I had managed to secure. Anyway, the climb to Sty Head went quickly, both of us bursting with rude health and radiating animal vigour. Look, this is my book, and if I want to indulge in the odd hyperbole, I will, OK? So we stand on the top of the pass, which is a major thoroughfare between Borrowdale and Wasdale, cleaved between the magnificent Great Gable scraping the sky on one side and, on the other, the shoulder running from the equally magnificent Great End to a somewhat less prepossessing, but graceful nevertheless, Seathwaite Fell. And we marvel at the breathtaking views. I wanted to tack the marvelling to the end of the previous sentence but decided I couldn't do this to you. So we stand there, mesmerised by the formidable gullies of the precipitous north face of Lingmell straight ahead and, to the left, by the lofty jagged ridge leading to Scafell Pike, the highest mountain in England. But we couldn't afford to stay mesmerised for long because we now needed to descend to Wasdale Head, which we could see low down in the distance.

Some six miles later, we are finally at the bottom, ready to commence our Wasdale ramble. I had decided that we were going to tackle the famous Screes walk, which would take us along the south-western shore of Wast Water. The route threaded its way right at the bottom of the famous screes tumbling dramatically down the steep slopes of Illgill Head and Whin Rigg. Cutting across Wasdale Head, we made for the lake, whose smooth surface acted as a perfect mirror for both fells that morning. It started promisingly enough: the lakeshore path was a delight and the slope to our left nicely grassy. But the further we went, the stonier the trail became until, eventually, it petered out completely, leaving us to leap from one boulder to another. Never a great leaper, I found the passage taxing to say the least, and I don't think Vinnie was too enamoured either, so it was with palpable relief that we finally reached the end of Wast Water. Never again!

Now in Nether Wasdale, we rounded the tip of the lake and reached the road leading to Wasdale Head. We had now covered ten miles yet barely done half of the walk. Well, I knew this, but Vinnie didn't. Thankfully, he agreed to my, somewhat feeble given the circumstances, suggestion that we consume our lunch while walking along the road. Although we hadn't had any breaks yet, I knew that if we stopped we wouldn't make the return bus. Obviously, there were no buses for us in Wasdale, so we first needed to climb out of the valley and then descend to Ennerdale. In those days, although only on Sundays in high season, we had this marvellous bus which started on the west coast, drove to Buttermere to pick up passengers from the first, early, bus from Keswick and then proceeded all the way to Bowness Knott. So I could actually reach Ennerdale by public transport – those were the heady days for the unmotorised!

You got there for 11am, and, like a stern class-mistress, the bus allowed you five hours – and no more – for your exploration before returning to pick you up at 4pm. No later, or indeed other, buses would venture there, and, if you missed this one, you faced the prospect of waiting till the following Sunday to be rescued. And, for us, these were still pre-mobile-phone days.

So I am trying to set a brisk pace, and we are speeding along this road while eating our lunch, with me doing my best not to choke on my nuts. You see, I'm very health conscious and, as such, an avid follower of Dr Michael Moseley. And Dr Michael Moseley says to eat nuts. So I eat nuts. Actually, I have read that, if I did that, I stood a decent chance of achieving immortality. Honestly! All those health articles telling you that if you followed a healthy diet you were less likely to die. And nuts were an integral part of a healthy diet. I don't know about you, but I find this scientific discovery most heartening. Mind you, if we all lived forever, think what would happen to our beleaguered NHS. Then again, with the promised colossal benefits of Brexit just round the corner… although, in his pre-knighthood days, Sir Jacob Rees-Mogg quite openly admitted that it would be some fifty years before these benefits could be felt by ordinary folk. But, because we'll live forever, we should be absolutely fine: what's fifty years in the face of eternity? Besides, regaining your sovereignty is far more important than being able to pay your mortgage. Or your rent. Or your care-home fees. Then again, he obviously thought that sovereignty was for little people. Because, after the Brexit vote, he set up a fund management company in Dublin. Which is in the Irish Republic. Which is in in the EU (we mustn't say this too loudly, though). Because an unfettered access to its vast market would net the company a lot of lovely moolah. And he is not the only one. But they are all millionaires, so they are a special case.

Anyway, you won't be surprised that one as enamoured of nuts as I am felt compelled to compose a little ode to them.

> Nuts are very good for you –
> Here's a handy overview:
> They contain Omega 3s,
> Helpful for arthritic knees,
>
> And are said to be a measure
> Which 'protects one from blood pressure',
> Though I've always understood
> *Some* blood pressure to be good…
>
> Anyway, that's by the by;
> On the whole, one can't deny
> They are bundles of perfection
> That may combat an infection,
>
> Keep the Monster C at bay,
> And make sure one's heart's OK;
> They can even fight depression
> And aid microbe non-aggression.
>
> Health-wise, then, they are a must,
> After which I always lust;
> While I wouldn't want to brag,
> Every day, I get a bag

> Of pistachios – yum, yum, yum –
> But its warning is so dumb
> (I wish I could see your faces):
> 'This may well contain nut traces'!

OK, OK, so my ode may contain a little sting in the tail, but I am not a comic writer for nothing.

After some two miles of road-walking, we finally reached Nether Beck and started ascending up the long Netherbeck Valley, our path leading to the high pass separating Scoat Fell from Haycock. I certainly wouldn't recommend undertaking this climb after walking for twelve or so miles already. And I don't know about you, but when I roam, a song often pops into my head, and then I can't get it out and hum as I go. The one which decided to settle in my brain on that particular occasion was *I Need a Hero* by Bonnie Tyler. I have no idea why: after all, I had always been struck by its absurdity. What modern woman needs a hero these days? We are not at war. I know, I know, the song is supposed to be tongue-in-cheek, but you can't be too careful. After all, people can be easily influenced. Particularly when they are young and impressionable. I know of a young man who was dreaming of performing heroic deeds to impress his girlfriend. Honestly. Tell him to offer her to do his share of domestic chores. That would impress her all right, I can tell you.

> I don't need a hero; the notion's absurd –
> A knight, with his shine, will not have me stirred.
> The man I would like? No, never a groover;
> Instead, he's a bloke au fait with a hoover.

I don't need a hero; the notion's insane –
What good is a dragon that has just been slain?
My wish list includes a practical guy
Who's good rustling up lamb shanks & kale pie.

I don't need a hero; please don't make me laugh –
Defender of honour? You're joking – not half!
A duster is never a thing of my choice:
A wielder thereof would make me rejoice.

I don't need a hero; that's silly – all right?
I'd rather have someone who gets up at night
To change a soiled nappy, give babies their feed;
Now, this is the bloke I know I might need.

I don't need a hero; it's foolish – I've said;
A guy I would rate won't hide in his shed –
Instead, he will be my emotional crutch
And talk about feelings – that's all (it's not much).

I don't need a hero? Hang on just a sec –
The bloke I've described: he does fit the spec!

Well, all right then: I'm too old for babies and nappies, but everything else is spot on.

So we plodded on, Vinnie in stony silence and I humming the tune of this idiotic song until, at long last, we reached the pass.

"So where is this bus stop, then?" There was no mistaking the annoyance in his voice, his usual equanimity having patently deserted him.

"E-r-r-r-r, it's there."

"*Where?*"

"There, there." I pointed to the far end of the long valley stretching out at our feet.

"Bloody hell; but it's miles away!"

And so it was, some 4.5 miles from where we were standing. Given that Vinnie had no option of refusing to go any further, we commenced our long descent wearily. I even stopped humming. Finally, we reached the bottom of the valley, but there was still quite a distance to cover. And our bus was leaving in less than half an hour. After some twenty miles and ten hours on the go – *with no stops* – I was now wilting and knew that we wouldn't make it. (Little wonder that I have knackered my hip, but that particular story will come a bit later.) Vinnie, however, must have got his tenth wind (having exhausted all his previous ones), for he said he was going to run and dashed off. Honestly, I had never seen anyone sprint with such velocity. I've told you about my racing for the last bus in Great Langdale, haven't I? No comparison, no comparison at all.

I finally reached Bowness Knott after the bus's departure time, pained that Vinnie's valiant effort was in vain. But hold on: the bus was still there, waiting for me – unbelievable! And this lovely Cumbrian driver wasn't the only helpful one I have come across over the years by any means, so the picture wasn't nearly as gloomy as that painted in the two previous chapters. Since then, however, whenever I told Vinnie that we were off for a nice walk, he would shoot me a highly suspicious look and demand to see the map.

Before I finish, I have another apposite Ennerdale tale for you. On another Sunday in high season, my dear friends Patti (sadly, no longer with us) and Bobby and I had to return on the same Bowness Knott bus. Previously, we had kept meeting on the buses and bumping into one another on the fells until, eventually, we became good pals and started doing some walks together.

I had introduced them to this brilliant bus, which I had generously forgiven for limiting us to five hours' worth of Ennerdale exploration only. But, to us then, it was enough to climb Haycock, soaring high above the valley bottom. Having conquered our mountain, we were descending when Bobby needed to hang back to commune with nature for a bit. Unfortunately, the communing was going to take place before a crossroads. Unthinkingly, I went past, knowing Ennerdale like the back of my hand. But Bobby didn't. Finding himself abandoned in an unfamiliar place, he somehow managed to get to the bus stop along a different route, although it entailed wading through high water – what an intrepid man! There, he explained our predicament to the driver, already poised for departure. In the meantime, my frantic shouts to him went unanswered, so I told Patti to continue to Bowness Knott and went back looking for him. He then went looking for me, whereupon Patti went looking for both of us. When we all found each other and ran for the bus, it was still waiting for us – half an hour after its scheduled departure time! But that's not all: the bus was going only as far as Buttermere (where we were supposed to change for the last Keswick bus) before heading back to the west coast, but, of course, there was now no chance of our making the connection. So the lovely driver asked the passengers whether they minded if he drove all the way to Keswick – just for the three of us (everyone else on board was, evidently, from the west coast)! In unison, the equally lovely ramblers approved the rescue mission, and the vehicle, laden with its good-natured cargo, took us home. How about *that*?

>A bus driver in the Lakes
>Is endowed with what it takes:
>Sells you tickets, gives advice,
>Sometimes whistles (which is nice),
>Navigates our narrow roads,
>Dodging vans and heavy loads,
>Not to mention tractors, which
>Try to force him in the ditch;
>Always measured, never rash,
>And, on seeing your mad dash
>(You are late from your long roam),
>Waits for you and takes you home!

A slightly younger Anna — but the sparkle in her eyes remains the same

Anna on Bessyboot (Rosthwaite Fell), 2022

Anna with her lovely Skiddaw u3a Roamers on Loughrigg Fell, 2022

Anna with Vinnie by Dock Tarn, 2022

Anna with her lovely Skiddaw u3a Roamers on the misty High Tove, 2022

Anna and Vinnie after the group walk celebrating her 70th birthday, 2022

Anna with her lovely Skiddaw u3a Roamers by Harrop Tarn, 2022

Anna with Bobby on Surprise View above Derwentwater, 2022

Anna with Bobby by Ruthwaite Lodge (of the poppy-seed-cake tale), 2022

Anna on the summit of the very misty Scafell, 2023

Anna on the summit of Steeple, 2023

Anna on the summit of Wasdale Red Pike, her final Wainwright fell in the ninth round, 2023

Anna with her lovely Skiddaw u3a Roamers on the summit of Blake Fell, 2023

Anna with her lovely Skiddaw u3a Roamers on the misty summit of Raven Crag, 2023

Anna with her lovely Skiddaw u3a Roamers on the summit of Black Fell, 2023

Anna with her lovely Skiddaw u3a Roamers on the summit of Dodd, 2023

10

Writer's Block and My Skiddaw Rescue

Given that I live in the Lake District, my exploits are not limited to warmer months. No, afficionados such as me walk all year round. And the January weather in that particular year had been grim. We'd had downpours, gales, snow, ice and extreme cold. Yet, in those days, I was quite prepared to brave the elements in all seasons. Besides, pitting yourself against Mother Nature is an excellent way of overcoming frustration. And I was full of frustration: I had been suffering from writer's block. Because my Lady Muse had deserted me. Perhaps I shouldn't have retired the Polish one: we Poles are very reliable.

> We've just had a bust-up, see,
> My neglectful Muse and me
> 'Cos she wants – you won't believe –
> Even *more* by way of leave.

What a cheek! But it's no use
Having bust-ups with my Muse,
For, however much I scoff,
She is always swanning off

And refusing to play ball.
You don't like these rhymes at all?
In that case, please hear my plea:
Blame my Muse – and pity me!

After I had remonstrated with her, she came straight out with it: apparently, I wasn't worth wasting time on. Chagrined, I showed her the poem below, but she just shrugged her shoulders and said that she was going on strike to demand better working conditions. She was, clearly, well ahead of the curve there, wasn't she? I did try to put a greatly improved offer on the table, but she would have none of it, brutally adding that I would never make the grade. Well, if she couldn't appreciate my poetic efforts, I might have to start looking for a replacement. And I am consoling myself with the hope that your verdict may be a little kinder, you being possessed of a highly refined literary taste (the second clause being the so-called absolute construction – as, indeed, is this one).

Storm is raging, world's aswirl,
Trees all tremble, bushes curl,
Chimney thunders and pipes wail
In this mighty roaring gale.

What's this spidery silhouette
Doing twirly pirouette?
Honeysuckle, freed at last
By the wind's almighty blast?

Amid turbulence and din,
Angry heavens have caved in
Pounding vulnerable Earth,
Wildly swaying in its berth.

For the time being, though, I felt that I had no option but to abandon all attempts at highbrow poetry. So, frustrated, I donned my winter-walking gear, grabbed my rucksack and went climbing.

Skiddaw is a magnificent mountain overtopping Keswick. At 3,054 feet (see, I didn't say 931 metres! How's that for total assimilation?), it is the fourth highest fell in the Lake District. It's so close to my house that, strictly speaking, I can climb straight up it without using any form of transport to the start of the walk, but, on that occasion, I decided to take the bus so that I could mount my attack from Cockup (yes, it's a name, not a joke) right at the back, near Bassenthwaite. The gloominess of the sagging sky didn't bode well for the enterprise, but I hadn't, evidently, acquired sufficient sense by then.

So I get off the bus at the end of Orthwaite Road and try to follow it, slipping and sliding as I go, for the minor road is iced over. At Melbecks, I turn towards the wide white slope, much of its bulk disappearing into the cloud. Because of the snow blanketing the ground, the going is hard already, and I haven't even begun climbing yet. But, hey, I've started, so I'll finish. I find a more accessible-looking section between two steeper ones and start ascending, sinking deeper and deeper into the snow with every step. Needless to say, there is no trace of a path anywhere because everything is covered in a thick white blanket. And there are no footsteps to be discerned in any direction. After all, it's 29 January, the snow has been falling heavily for the past few days, it's blowing a hooley and sensible people have better things to do in such weather. I now have no visibility at all but try to buoy myself up by reminding myself that I know the terrain well and that I will be fine as soon as I get to the fence running from Dash Falls all the way up to near the summit of Skiddaw. But it's no fun to keep going when you are stuck in the snow to above your knees and can't see anything around you. If I'd had a car waiting for me at the back of Skiddaw, I would have turned back. At least I hope I would have. But I didn't. So I staggered on.

You know that I like cheering myself up, don't you? And, sometimes, I find that comparing my predicament to an even trickier one helps a little. Remember my Mardale Head adventure? I thus cast my mind back to when I had found myself in an even more dicey situation. I was in the Rila Mountains in Bulgaria, the highest mountain range in the country. By myself. And I didn't know the area at all. It was Easter and I had decided to do a route I had found in a guidebook, which involved an overnight stay in a mountain bothy apparently run by a local hiking club. The bridleway leading along the valley bottom was easy to follow, but I then had to start ascending up a slope all the way to the ridge high above. And the slope was covered in thick snow, which grew deeper the higher I went. My progress was thus snail-slow, and it started getting dark. Where was this blasted bothy? I was straining my eyes, but all I could see was the whiteness of the snow all around and the darkness of the sky above. I was now up to mid-thigh in. I started yelling for help (in Bulgarian, but I'm sure that screams are, in similar circumstances, understood right across all languages). No response. I stopped when I shouted myself hoarse. I also gave up trying to pull each leg out and, half-in, rested my torso on the snow. Well, I will probably go to sleep, and, if I wake up, I wake up and, if I don't…

Somehow, I managed to motivate myself to have one more look around. Wait, wait, what's this angular shape? The one higher up, faintly delineated against the sky. With a sudden surge of energy, I somehow extricated myself and started crawling upwards, trying to spread myself as wide as possible to prevent myself from sinking too deeply into the snow. It was a mountain hut! What a relief. There was no sign of life anywhere: it was obvious that there was nobody about. After all, I couldn't see even a flicker of light or discern any footsteps in the pristine snow. But it didn't matter: I knew that I would survive the night. I grabbed a stone lying nearby and smashed a window to get in. The hut was, indeed, abandoned, but it had bunk beds with lots of blankets on them. When I tried to lift the blankets, I could feel that they were damp: the hut cannot have had any heating for a while. And they weighed an absolute ton: it must have been the dampness. I then noticed blood on my hands, but I didn't care. After all, I didn't feel any pain. Funny what adrenaline does to you. Fully clothed, I crawled under the blankets and fell asleep.

It was already light when I woke up. I got up and surveyed my surroundings. The hut looked very much like the uninhabited Mosedale Cottage in the Lake District's Far Eastern Fells: a few tables, chairs and shelves, a fireplace which, clearly, hadn't seen any action for a while with some firewood stacked up beside it, some cooking utensils, cutlery and crockery and I forget what else. I walked up to the door and turned the handle. The door offered no resistance: it was unlocked. Oh, no: I had not needed to smash the window at all! I felt awful, but there was nobody to apologise to. I went out onto the porch and… was dazzled. It was a very sunny day, and the sparkling whiteness of the mountains, which could be seen for miles and miles around, was spell-binding in its brilliance. What an incredible sight! Don't forget that these were very high mountains, far higher than our Lakeland fells, so, even though it was Easter already, they were still sporting their full winter garb. Regrettably, I myself hadn't appreciated this when I was planning my hike – if planning is the correct term for my reckless adventure. Mesmerised, I sat on the porch and slowly finished the food I had left. As I was being enthralled, I remembered an equally dazzling early morning in the Lakes, although our mountains were not blanketed by snow then.

> Early morning, crisp and bright,
> And the summits are alight
> As the sun, with sleepy yawns,
> Raises while the new day dawns.

Then it shakes its golden hair,
Stretches, laughs without a care,
Dissipating morning haze,
And the mountains stand ablaze.

Eventually, I had to stir but knew that this incredible vision would stay with me forever. So far, it's been forty-five years: I was very young then. Needless to say, I had no intention of continuing with my foolhardy expedition and decided to retrace my steps – which was easy, what with my footsteps clearly imprinted onto the otherwise undisturbed snow. On my way down, albeit only a short distance away, I spotted a proper mountain bothy: the guidebook must have meant that one. Although its door was locked, there was a cat on the windowsill inside, and the bothy was clearly lived in. Whoever was running it must have decided to take an Easter break. I didn't think people were supposed to abandon mountain refuges advertised as open all the year round: what if hikers needed them to shelter for the night – I did, after all – and it was all locked up? This would never have happened in our Tatras. But maybe they were using this hut as a back-up. Or had never come across an idiot such as me. You do all sorts of stupid things when you are young, though. I mean, not you *personally*, obviously.

Returning to my Skiddaw adventure (or should it be lunacy?), I am now staggering through the deep snow up this vast slope, which probably belongs to Bakestall, Skiddaw's northern satellite. Trying not to fall into the ravine of Dead Beck (did they really have to give it this particular name?), I finally reach the fence. Phew! All I need to do now is press for, and clear, the summit because Keswick, and salvation, are on the other side. As I go up, there is progressively less snow on the exposed slope because the gale has blown much of it off. But the wind is vicious. Just get to the summit, just get to the summit. On my hands and knees, I reach the slatey top, too windswept for any snow to cling to it, and start descending onto the other side. Soon, however, the snow reappears: this slope is more protected from the wind. I descend to what I'm guessing is the depression between the summit of Skiddaw and the top of Skiddaw Little Man (there is nothing little about this particular man, though) – there is still no visibility. Suddenly, I find myself inside a giant milk bottle, completely enveloped in whiteness. On all sides. I don't know where the ground finishes and the sky begins. The lovely natives call it a whiteout, and I can only hope that you will never experience it. Disorientated, I step on something hard. It's the top of a fence, protruding no more than one or two inches from a deep snowdrift. Where does this fence go? Where does this fence go? I should have known: I had climbed Skiddaw dozens and dozens of times. But, in my increasing panic, I couldn't think straight. So I try to follow the top of the fence, but it doesn't seem to be descending as low as I need it to.

Confused, I go back. Then I make a bid to abandon this fence altogether, but now I truly don't know where I am. After staggering round in circles for goodness knows how long, I retrace my steps and return to the fence. But it's now after 3.30pm, and I am rapidly running out of daylight. After all, it's 29 January. So I pull out my mobile and try to call the mountain rescue. Not easy when your fingers are so cold that they can hardly grip, but I finally succeed in calling 999. The rescuers tell me to stick to the fence. But, if I do, I'll die of hypothermia: if I am where I think I am, my altitude is still about 2,500 feet. Anyway, I don't need to know my altitude to be aware that I'm very cold. I thus feel I have no choice but to descend further. Given the depth of the snow, the best way is to slide on my posterior. Thankfully, I have enough lucidity to realise that to go right is to meet certain death, the mountain's western slope being precipitous. So it has to be left. I thus begin my slide. Do you know how fast you can accelerate when you slide down a steepish snow-blanketed slope? I didn't. But I do now: *very* fast indeed. Suddenly realising that my descent is in danger of getting out of control, I start digging my heels in furiously – I had no ice-axe – in order to slow it down. It works! I land somewhere at the bottom, where I am sheltered from the wind. Phew: at least I may avoid hypothermia. For what seems like ages, I sit there in total darkness: there is no flicker of light anywhere, this side of Skiddaw facing away from any human habitation. Admittedly, I have two torches on me, but they are only small, so I can't identify anything sitting further than a few feet away. And, as I'm hunkering down, I have to take my mind off my predicament somehow. Valentine's Day is just around the corner, so why not compose a little verse for the occasion?

> If you aren't in a pair,
> It's a rather sad affair:
> All these hearts and fluffy stuff
> Make this jamboree quite tough;

It's a fest of coupledom,
Glorified on *Love.com*;
But reflect on it a tad,
It is really not that bad;

First, there is a perk of note:
A control of one's remote,
Which is sole and absolute;
You may wish to switch to mute,

You may channel-surf at will,
You may gorge on sport and chill,
Watch a thriller or a weepie
Or delight in something creepy.

You may also, on a whim,
Fly to Tonga for a swim,
Go skydiving in Dubai
With no need for a goodbye,

Or hang-gliding in Japan
Without flouting any ban;
You may even, if you wish,
Dedicate yourself to fish.

You may dye your hair bright red
Or play solitaire in bed,
Relocate to the Bahamas
Or – just veg in your pyjamas.

Trust me, you will do just fine
Sans a special Valentine,
And, besides, there's every chance
Of tomorrow's hot romance.

Then you'll really have a blast,
But, when several years have passed,
Some of you may feel undone,
Musing, freedom was such fun!

Suddenly, what's this? Could this be a light? Yes, and more than one! In fact, it's several lights moving in the distance. At last! Now they have merged, forming a river of light, and this river flows upwards towards the fence I had slid down from. Facing the lights, I stand up, my head torch on, and start furiously waving my other torch. The river of light stops at the top and then, in a straight line, starts flowing down directly towards me. It had to be in a straight line: even if the rescuers hadn't seen my torchlights, they couldn't have missed the groove made in the snow by my rear end. It's 7pm when they get to me. One of my saviours quickly pulls out what looks like a large cape and, with a swift circular motion, forms a makeshift tent around several of us. They check out my boots and clothes and give me a chocolate bar. Meanwhile, I'm busy crying and apologising. Wouldn't you be crying out of sheer embarrassment and apologising for inconveniencing these wonderful people because of your own stupidity?

It turns out that they are the Cockermouth Mountain Rescue Team. They ask me if I can walk, and I say yes. So we all walk back to their vehicle, parked quite a distance away. Apparently, I landed somewhere behind Skiddaw House, so we can use the bridleway called the Cumbria Way. It takes us past Dash Falls and down into the valley – not that I can see much. To make things worse, they tell me that there is another mountain rescue team looking for me: that from Keswick, apparently ascending up Jenkin Hill. Imagine my mortification! When all those brilliant people could be sitting by the blazing fire and sipping nice brandy. I get back home at 9pm – twelve hours after my reckless escapade began.

The promise I made to myself then was to learn to turn back when the going got too rough. In the main, I have kept this promise, although there have been a few more close shaves.

> January, some years back,
> I received a lot of flak
> When I blundered – went astray –
> On a freezing winter's day.
>
> Gale was howling, snow was deep,
> Skiddaw's slopes rose white and steep,
> With its summit in the cloud,
> But I planned my climb, unbowed,
>
> Pining for the lofty top
> With no image of a flop.
> I was soon, despite the freeze,
> Crawling on my hands and knees

Yet still sinking in the snow,
With my progress very slow;
But, regardless, on I pressed,
Which (in case you haven't guessed)

Was a reckless thing to do
Given that nobody knew
Where I was on this vast slope;
Yep, I acted like a dope.

Upwards, higher, then – a fright:
The world went completely white!
There was nothing I could see,
So, as startled as can be,

I did rummage for my phone
And, in a hysteric tone,
Called the mountain rescue, who
Mobilised our local crew

And another team as well;
One then got me off the fell –
Now in darkness: 'twas pitch black,
With no trace of any track.

I was, clearly, in those days
Still in my immortal phase;
Now, with whiteout on the tops,
I stay low and hit the shops!

That day did mark the end of my immortal phase, though. But, for several years afterwards, I made a point of climbing Skiddaw on 29 January – albeit in better weather. Then I thought, *why? Why am I doing this? What am I trying to prove?* So I stopped.

This has been my short dramatic interlude, by the way; after all, there wasn't anything uproariously funny about that day. Besides, it shows that I can do dramatic. But I couldn't finish this chapter without a paean to our wonderful mountain rescue teams, could I?

> Mountain rescue gals and boys
> Never, ever lose their poise
> When a walker's out of luck
> And is somewhere badly stuck.
>
> You are lost, it's getting late;
> They will help you navigate –
> That is, if you're in one piece,
> And your mobile did not cease.
>
> But if you're stricken, cannot move,
> They will never disapprove
> And will climb to any height,
> In all weathers, day or night.
>
> They will cope with rough terrain
> Just to ease the victim's pain
> And revive those out of it:
> They do carry all the kit;

They will splinter broken bones
Shattered on protruding stones
And will get you safely down;
You are grateful they're around.

Mountain rescue gals and boys
Never, ever lose their poise,
Neither do they lose control
When this walker is a Pole!

11

Men, Philosophy and Ruthwaite Lodge in Grisedale

In general, I'm in favour of men. I really am. I mean, all this stuff about toxic masculinity, honestly. It must be quite upsetting for them. So I have penned this little verse to cheer them up. Well, maybe not the guy who wouldn't dismount from his bike on the Portinscale footbridge and sternly demanded that I go back to my *own* country. Forthwith.

> Men have had bad press of late –
> Let me set the record straight:
> Males can build a GPS
> And dispense a warm caress,
>
> Wield a spanner and a spear
> And explore the stratosphere,
> Fix the car so it won't splutter,
> Paint the fence and clear the gutter.

Guys are good at felling trees,
Which they manage with great ease,
Not to mention drilling holes,
Flying planes and heading balls.

Males can master Ancient Greek,
And perfect the gap technique,
Split the atom, swing the axe,
And invent the income tax.

Men can go pursue blue whales
And are very good with nails,
Can erect a chimney stack
And adeptly ride a yak.

Blokes can hunt wild boar and grouse
And expunge a nuisance mouse;
They can also drill for oil
And restore an old gargoyle,

Although some are less than happy
When confronted with a nappy;
Nappies aren't accidental:
There, men have been instrumental.

Guys can wrestle with a bear
And eat fire for a dare,
Manufacture steel and soap
And could even be the Pope,

> Plus, are never daunted either
> Having to evict a spider.
> I won't keep this confidential:
> Men are, clearly, an essential!

The men I know are really nice. Adam, Alan, Andrew, Brian, Clive, Julian, Nicky, Paul, Robin and Stuart, to name but a few (in a strictly alphabetical order to forestall any squabbles) – they are all lovely. And, of course, Bobby. I think I have said that he is our dear friend, haven't I? But what I haven't told you is that he is American.

> He is from the USA,
> Though this can't be helped, OK?
> He's loved all the same,
> And Bob is his name,
> "Great bloke," is what we all say.

As you can clearly see from the above, Vinnie and I have never held his nationality against him: you can't help where you are born, can you? Look at me. Actually, no, no, don't look at me. I'm seventy, for goodness' sake, with things sagging, drooping and falling off. Reaching this milestone was so traumatic that even therapy didn't help. I used the same therapist I had engaged after I had left FART. Only, on this occasion, I needed thirty one-hour sessions. And it still didn't work. *And* she had put up her prices. There had to be a better way. The only thing for it was to compose a little verse.

There must be – *must* be – some mistake:
Seventy candles on the cake?
How did this happen? As you say,
Your zenith was but yesterday.

This was the time of your fab youth
When politicians told the truth,
The country rocked and swung and swayed
And Europe didn't make the grade.

You wore flared trousers, drank whiskey neat,
The worst you did was run through wheat,
OK, maybe you smoked a joint,
All harmless fun – which was the point.

Those mods and rockers were so cool,
Their leather jackets made you drool,
And yours was such a joyous grin
When England clinched the World Cup win.

You ate pork pies, good English grub,
And spent your lunchtimes in the pub,
Had Sunday roasts – no foreign muck:
Moroccan koftas? Simply yuck!

Your hopes were high and barriers low,
You planned to earn a lot of dough,
To operate in overdrive
And to be free by forty-five.

Your yesterday – it was so fine!
Still, dear old Reg (he's ninety-nine)
Does call you 'young 'un' (what a sage)
And sighs: "I wish I were your age…"

The man I've done the most walks with is Bobby. By a mile. And not just by one mile. Over the years, we have covered countless and had many adventures. Inexplicably, he seems to have escaped relatively unscathed by the experience. But I like walking with him because not only is he an excellent rambler, but he is also very clever: he has a doctorate in philosophy.

There once was this great bloke called Bobby,
Who used to read Greek for a hobby,
From Latin he'd quote,
Knew French words of note,
And yet he was not at all snobby.

And his philosophicalness (I wanted to write philosophicality, but my Oxford English Dictionary – which boasts twenty volumes, all of which I proudly possess – says it's philosophicalness) seems to have rubbed off on me – albeit only a tiny bit. But even such a negligible amount has been enough to enable me to pen all these profoundly philosophical verses. Well, you will be the best judge of the profundity of this one.

The trouble with verse,
Long, medium or terse,
Is as follows: it has to be written;

My words are my tools,
But there are no rules
How to make all one's readers quite smitten.

Some think it a crime
When poems don't rhyme –
I do not (nor does Roger McGough),
That said, all mine do,
It's easy? Not true:
It takes time – I can't just dash them off.

Now, this is the thing:
My verses must sing,
So I sweat to make sure that they scan;
The rhythm's not right?
I need to re-write
Or my ditty may go down the pan.

I know I'm no bard,
It's, though, rather hard
When English is more yours than mine;
Though I am enthralled,
My progress has stalled:
Will I make it by eighty and nine?

Yet – what does this mean?
I'd better come clean:
Being read does appear to be heady;
But mine's a good life,
Sans crises or strife,
So I guess I have made it already…

Bobby and I have even created our own Easter ritual. Which involved a bus, as Bobby no longer drove. Without this bus, we unmotorised Keswickians would have had to go through Penrith to get to Patterdale in the eastern Lakes, which is our gateway to many fabulous walks. But, with the advent of the summer season, Stagecoach lays on this fantastic bus that goes directly from Keswick to Patterdale. So, rather than wasting two hours in transit, we can get to Patterdale in forty minutes. Brilliant! Unfortunately, however, the bus runs only on Saturdays. In the past, it was more frequent, but Stagecoach evidently wasn't satisfied with the quantity of the passengers using it, so they killed it. I did say no dough – no dice, didn't I? So, these days, our summer Saturdays are sacrosanct. Unsurprisingly, we locals pile onto this bus as soon as it starts running. You won't believe the friendships I've made on it. But you can meet all sorts of interesting people on any bus. Like this man with a clarinet, for example.

> The man with a clarinet –
> He's the one I have just met:
> I was sitting on the bus
> With my Vinnie; both of us
> Were just gazing at the view,
> Appreciating it anew,
> For the beauty of the fells
> Casts all sorts of wondrous spells;
>
> It was quiet: other folk
> Watched their phones, and no one spoke;
> Then we hear this lovely sound,

We all start and look around;
Here he is: a bearded guy
With a twinkle in his eye
Playing an enchanting tune:
We all smile and clap and swoon

And then start to hum and sing,
All infected by his zing;
He then plays some more, and we
All surrender to our glee;
Marvel: at the journey's end
Everyone has found a friend;
You would love him (wanna bet?) –
The man with a clarinet.

Back to the Patterdale bus. You know that Easter Saturday always falls on a Saturday, don't you? And Easter, fortunately, always happens during the summer season. This means that, on Easter Saturday, we can get to Patterdale on this fantastic bus. And, by a happy coincidence, it is also when they open Ruthwaite Lodge in Grisedale. The lodge sits high in the valley on the edge of Ruthwaite Cove, encircled by stern-looking crags. It had, apparently, been a hunter's refuge before becoming a climbing hut. The lodge is usually shut, but, at Easter, it throws open its door in aid of Macmillan Cancer Support. So our annual Easter ritual is to visit the lodge and support the charity. You won't believe the refreshments they offer! But, first, we have to get to it.

We thus get off at Patterdale and start ascending along the bottom of Grisedale. And, straight ahead of us, rises the shapely pyramid of Falcon Crag perching on the side of the lofty Dollywaggon Pike, which itself stands on the main spine of the Helvellyn range. Higher up, the valley is flanked by the steep slope of St Sunday Crag on one side and, on the other, by a ridge tumbling down from an even loftier Nethermost Pike, Helvellyn's next-door neighbour.

Obviously, we are not the only ones heading for the lodge. In fact, there is a whole crowd of us, everyone being propelled by the prospect of delicious treats on offer. Their poppy seed cake is out of this world. Actually, that's what we used to have in Poland on Christmas Eve, which is when our main Christmas celebrations take place. Ah, our Polish Christmases! They used to be much more low-key than the British jamboree but were delightful nevertheless. Before I become too weepy, however, I must share with you my deeply-held belief that, in order to become truly British, one must do Christmas the British way. So here is our approximation of a British Christmas. Obviously, it's not up to me to judge the extent to which it resembles the real thing; that will be done by you.

> 'Tis a magic time of year,
> Time of gladness, joy and cheer,
> When folk love to have a fete,
> Eat and drink and celebrate.
>
> In our house, we too, as one,
> Had a most tremendous fun,
> Though there was, I do declare,
> The odd hiccup here and there,

Such as all the rigmarole
With the toad in his wee hole;[1]
Turkey? Raw inside (oh, drat!),
So we gave it to the cat;

Roast potatoes, I must say,
Went a rather different way:
Badly burnt and hard as rock
(Not that we would ever squawk);

Veggies having turned to slime,
Guests jumped up: "Is that the time?!"
"Nonsense!" we'd then gaily shout,
"Won't you have another sprout?"

Christmas pud would have been handy,
But we'd guzzled all the brandy;
As for pies – this makes me wince –
Uncle'd eaten all the mince.

Radio playing *Silent Night*,
Both drunk cousins had a fight,
Kids got into awful scraps
Tearing off their present wraps,

And our dearest auntie Lyn
Sat there swigging rum and gin
With a rather mournful gaze:
"It was different in them days."

---

[1] How the lovely natives manage to squeeze the animal into a small hole is beyond me: my repeated attempts ended in abject failure, though, mercifully, the creature survived…

> Our granny, though, was merry,
> Having finished all the sherry,
> Then she swayed and, with a slouch,
> Was now snoring on the couch.
>
> All in all, as you can guess,
> Christmas was a great success,
> Though the fairy on the top
> Shut her eyes and shouted, "Stop!"
>
> But the day, this much is clear,
> Is the highlight of our year,
> So we cry, with joyous glow,
> "Only fifty weeks to go!"[2]

But our very British Christmas is still some way off, and, in the meantime, we are approaching Ruthwaite Lodge with its divine poppy seed cake. Regrettably, poppy seed cake is as rare in Britain as a non-motorist, but I adore it, so you can imagine what happens when we get to the lodge. Bobby and I settle ourselves down on one of the nice benches outside, and I go in and get myself a slice of poppy seed cake. (And they are big slices.) Bliss! So I go in and get myself another slice. Ecstasy! So I then go in and get myself a third slice. Heaven on Earth! But, hang on, hang on, what's this funny feeling in my tummy? Oh dear… Clutching my stomach, I stagger into the lodge to see if they have any Gaviscon. They don't. So all I can do is keep clutching my poor stomach.

---

[2] Well, maybe fifty-two, but who is counting after all this prosecco – pardon me, champagne.

Meanwhile, Bobby, being possessed of extraordinary willpower, purchases his slice, wraps it in a tissue and puts it in his rucksack. Having saved his cake for later (the concept I've never been able to grasp), he then looks at me and puts forth an unfathomable proposition: I would want to get some cake for Vinnie, surely. I wish! The man has clearly failed to appreciate that Vinnie's cake would have never survived the journey home intact. In fact, it wouldn't have survived the journey home full stop, however violent the protestations of my poor battered tummy.

> I don't cook, nor do I bake,
> But I'm crazy about cake,
> And what one so often needs
> Is nice cake with poppy seeds.
>
> Poppy seeds ensconced in dough
> Are my paradise, you know,
> Not because – here comes a quip –
> What I want's an opium trip!

And, just when you might have thought I was the pits: I may not cook as such (as per the above tale about my ruined Christmas turkey, potatoes and other veggies), but I do steam. To preserve vitamin C. We live on steamed fish and vegetables. Although there is no vitamin C in fish. But the Japanese also live on fish and vegetables, and look what a spectacular result: they go on forever. Then again, they probably eat everything raw. Come to think of it, so do I. Obviously, not *literally* everything, poppy seed cake being the notable exception. But perfection is boring. And seeds are good for your anyway. I've already told you of my love of nuts, but what I haven't told you yet is that it is equalled by my fondness for seeds. *All* seeds.

You can't imagine the fights I've been having with Vinnie. He always feeds the birds in our garden and buys these great big bags of bird seed for them. Yum, yum! So I always try to wrestle the bag off him to pinch at least some of the seeds for myself. He has now taken to hiding the bag. You won't believe some of his hiding places. I never thought the man had so much imagination. Obviously, I also buy my own seeds, but you can't have too much of a good thing. I guess I just don't have an off-switch for the stuff I like – which, thankfully, also includes fruit and veg.

> They do mean it when they say
> You must have your five a day
> Of the lovely fruit and veg,
> Which will give you quite an edge,
>
> Making you both fit and strong;
> Yet I feel they may be wrong:
> I don't think that I could thrive
> On the recommended five;
>
> You might deem me out of touch,
> But I eat *four* times as much,
> And this is precisely why
> I am permanently high,

With a grin from ear to ear –
Not a sight that would endear
Those who think themselves quite prim
And may reckon I am dim.

Do they know what's necessary
To make one's demeanour merry
From Kamchatka to Algeria?
Lots of friendly gut bacteria!

You want fruit and veg aplenty;
Take my counsel: go for twenty,
And remember, my good souls,
Give a miss to sausage rolls.

Protestations I'll pre-empt:
Poppy seeds are – yes! – exempt,
Even if they're in a cake
And result in bellyache!

Mind you, my incessant grinning had occurred before I turned seventy, but I seem to be on the road to recovery from the trauma, what with all the rabbit and bird food I consume. The poppy seed cake might also have played its therapeutic part. In addition to my ditties, of course: my verses always help. If I were you, I'd forget about therapists.

Anyway, we leave the lodge and continue up the valley. We reach the picturesque Grisedale Tarn, but rather than descending to the road on the other side, we scramble up the steep slope of Seat Sandal, which keeps a watchful eye over the tarn. To ease the pain, I promise

Bobby that once we've reached the summit, we can look forward to an easy descent down the fell's delightful southern shoulder, gently leading all the way to The Traveller's Rest in Grasmere. But I also hope to exorcise a recent, rather shameful, memory of an event which had contributed to my fall from grace. This, however, is the tale for another chapter. The job of this section was to set the scene and to whet your appetite.

But I have started this chapter with my musings about men, so, for the sake of symmetry, I feel I ought to offer you some further, profound, thoughts. Picture this scene: you are walking along a street in broad daylight and come upon this large yellow sign that says *men at work*. You like men at work very much, so, naturally, you make a beeline for them to show your appreciation.

> On seeing this sign, I hope you won't smirk:
> The one which proclaims that men are at work.
> You want some fresh air so go for a stroll,
> And there, in the street, you see a large hole.
>
> It's blocked by three vans, four cones and some tape,
> But where are the guys? Your mouth is agape,
> The board right in front – it quite clearly states
> It's road maintenance and does list the dates.
>
> You draw a bit nearer to survey the scene,
> And this is the picture you manage to glean:
> One large highway male is having a cig,
> His shovel pristine, not yet used to dig;

With his arms akimbo, another big bloke
Is ogling the females; this one is not woke;
His mate has his mobile glued right to his ear
And shouts kinds of stuff you don't want to hear;

Two guys in the cab (though slightly more blurred):
One's reading *The Sun* (if 'read' is the word),
Another tucks in – it looks like a pie;
But lunchtime has passed; you thus wonder why.

The sixth one, however, is right by the trench –
He's ready for action and wields a large wrench;
He spits in the hole and gives a big shrug:
"Them pipes are not right – there's more to be dug."

Indeed, time does pass, the hole does expand
And then it is filled – exactly as planned;
You must thus concede and give them their due:
These workmen do work – this much must be true.

12

Super-Spa, British Press, a Humble Supplication and the Keswick Refuse Debacle

Oops: having just confessed to my incessant high-spiritedness, I have failed to mention another one of its root causes. This omission, however, is about to get rectified. These days, we are swamped with all this healthy-living advice and bombarded with advertisements promising to boost our battered well-being and compromised mental health. We are assured that, for a mere ten grand a pop, we can get completely rejuvenated, renewed, revitalised, reinvigorated, restored, reanimated, regenerated and refreshed. Now look here, this tautological torrent isn't mine – it's theirs. All we need to do is book ourselves for treatment at their super-spa and bingo!

If you've got ten grand to spare,
They will gladly see you there,
At the super-spa which will
Detox you and make you chill.

There, their selling point of note
Is to be an antidote
To life's tensions, worries, strains;
It's a place where calmness reigns.

First, they make you ditch your phone,
And, however much you moan,
Remonstrate, or even cry,
You can't access their Wi-Fi.

They say Facebook's bad for you,
Twitter's evil through and through,
And, unless you are a doll,
Instagram won't help at all.

"Go cold turkey," they implore,
"And your spirits will then soar;
What will also give you highs
Is fresh air and exercise."

And, indeed, that's what you get,
Your exertions make you sweat,
But you do feel purified
Hiking through the countryside.

Then there's diet: veg and fruit
Make your viscera reboot,
With the berries quite a hit,
Strange as this is to admit.

No detoxing is complete
Until you foreswear red meat
And, in what is quite a leap,
Get eleven hours' sleep
(Disregarding the odd snooze)
And stay strictly off the booze.

All of this makes sense to me,
And I can't contain my glee
Because I could write a tome
On my doing this *at home* –
Out of doors, too – every day!
I thus save myself ten K!

Wouldn't you be incessantly high-spirited if you saved yourself ten grand (a pop) simply by following what is no more than good old-fashioned common sense? So that's my omission rectified. Actually, there is one more thing: you remember how I outwitted your border guards way back when? When I snuck into your country? So that's yet another reason for me to be cheery, although, admittedly, this avenue is not open to you. Then again, maybe you could try outmanoeuvring those darned Europeans when you travel on the continent…

On those occasions when I'm not rejuvenating, renewing, revitalising, reinvigorating, restoring, reanimating, regenerating and refreshing myself by hiking, I read. And not just about English grammar. I also love the British press – the refined variety, naturally. Isn't it simply superb? I mean the standard, the calibre, the sheer excellence! Reading quality broadsheets has been an education, I can tell you. So I devour them most avidly, expanding my horizons all the while. And, recently, I read about a revolutionary legal precedent that could prove transformative for countless folk the length and breadth of this country. Well, it might do if it were more widely known. I simply can't believe that nobody had reported it before. Thank goodness for *The Sunday Times*'s investigative prowess. On page eight of its 30th July 2023 issue came this revolutionary disclosure. Better late than never is what I say.

> *When Lisa Nandy's parents divorced at the age of seven, she realised home was more than just bricks and mortar.*

Hallelujah: no longer will the divorcing parents in Britain be bound by some stupid, arbitrarily-imposed, rule stipulating that they should be adults. But it's by no means the only extraordinary revelation I have come across. Far from it. In fact, I have been collecting similar gems for decades, culling them from the British press, radio, TV and other educated sources. Over said decades, I have amassed thousands of them: the shelves in my office are literally groaning under their weight. But, because I'm terrified of going on about English grammar and usage, I won't. After all, this topic had been proscribed in many British schools for decades until the noughties and still doesn't seem too popular generally. I can't, however, resist a small aside, being, as a rule, partial to asides of all sizes: the disregard for the study of grammar is another shock I had to absorb upon arriving on these welcoming shores. After all, grammar is the mortar which holds the lexical bricks together, organising language in a systematic way, and, as such, forms a part of general knowledge. So to see its importance dismissed by the educational establishment was a real eye-opener, and I'm truly chuffed that this important subject is back on the school curriculum.

Apropos proscription, I can't help thinking about the issue which nobody seems to dare mention these days. No, the subject of Brexit hasn't been banned, but the country has gone eerily quiet. Obviously, the Tories don't mention it because it has turned out to be an abject success, paving the way for Britain's world dominance, but have you noticed how deadly silent Labour has been on the subject? So everybody keeps shtum. I believe the lovely natives call it an elephant in the room, although how they imagine they could squash an elephant into a room rather baffles me. Unless it was a baby elephant… Anyway, I don't move in political circles, so I am entirely free to say that the result of the Brexit vote left me utterly flummoxed, bewildered and discombobulated. I mean, if you were me, wouldn't you wonder how it might affect your own situation? So here I am, utterly flummoxed, bewildered and discombobulated, wondering whether I might be turfed out. After all, the bloke who wouldn't dismount from his bike thought that I should be. If I were, how would I complete my next round of Wainwrights? Bummer! There was only one thing for it, namely composing a humble supplication. Which is exactly what I did.

Now that you've achieved your Brexit,
Please don't show me to the exit
'Cos, some misdeeds notwithstanding,
I could pass for quite upstanding

(Although not when in repose
After vodka overdose,
But I know that it is sinful
Having what you call a skinful):

I will not condone a fiddle
And sit roughly in the middle
On the scale from saints to sinners;
I eat carrots with my dinners,

Take crushed garlic, go for walkies,
Have foresworn soft-centre choccies,
And I'm also (fancy this!)
Upping my Omega 3s.

When I shop, I aways pay –
Even for my Beaujolais
And when I am sold a pup.
I believe in queuing up

(That's what Britons *always* do;
They are sticklers through and through);
I may shower every week,
Brush my gnashers when I reek;

Once a year, I dust my home,
I have even bought a gnome.
But there are (I'm shy, don't clap)
More fine feathers in my cap:

I have never been a chancer,
Smuggler, banker, spy, pole dancer
(Although I'm a dancing Pole);
I have tended to my soul

And renounced the deadly sins,[3]
And I've used recycling bins,
Plus, I *never* did striptease…
May I stay then? Pretty please!

It worked!

But, before I can explain what I have done with my reprieve (I call it a reprieve because you never know: after all, the likes of Nigel Farage, Arron Banks and Richard Trice are still about – not to mention the guy on the bike), I must tell you about our recycling bins. As I've just hinted, I'm very keen on recycling. Correction: we are. After all, anything to help our poor beleaguered Mother Earth – anything! So Vinnie and I had been using our recycling bins with utmost discipline, religiously sorting, segregating and separating our refuse before dumping it in separate receptacles. Until four months ago. Four months ago, our refuse collectors went on strike. Undoubtedly in solidarity with everyone else. It's not nice

---

3 Well, *at least* two of them.

being left out, is it? The bins in Keswick are overflowing, and I'm overcome with shame. No, no, I'm not one of these striking refuse collectors. I'm overcome with shame at my earlier pettiness. To complain about the odd missed bin, honestly. I can barely read the verse below without cringing. I'm quoting it here for the sake of balance. In the two verses above, I presented myself as a paragon, but even I have the odd character flaw, you know.

> You know I'm respectful and not one to diss,
> But these refuse guys – they've been so remiss:
> Our bin, full of waste, has been left by the kerb;
> Dereliction of duty that's bound to perturb:
>
> It will soon start to smell, and flies will descend,
> Plus, we pay for the service (a lot) in the end.
> It's called council tax, but what do we get?
> The lights are so dim we can't help but fret,
>
> The potholes are many, our buddies lament,
> Fair dos, we don't drive but cannot dissent,
> No kiddies at school (too old for that lark),
> And lots of dog poo all over the park,
>
> A precept for oldies – it won't touch the sides,
> (But this is the subject that irks and divides);
> As for the police, you may use this quote:
> "As rare as snow leopards and twice as remote."

The weeds are quite rampant and drains left uncleared,
And maintenance guys have all disappeared;
The least one can hope for, I swear on my sins,
Is for blokes in bright orange to empty one's bins.

I thus call the council, and they let me know
My call is important but queueing is slow;
They keep me on hold; I have sweaty palms:
They play horrid tunes – I wish it were Brahms.

An hour has passed, I wake up: a voice –
A human, a human! I had to rejoice;
She asked, "Can I help you?" – I told her she could:
"Just clear all my rubbish, oh, please, if you would."

"It's not my department," the voice did advise –
To scream at this point would not have been wise;
To give her her due, she did put me through,
But something went wrong: on hold – déjà vu;

Some more awful tunes: I wish I were deaf,
I nearly say something that starts with an F,
But then, at long last, I reach someone new:
This one is the right one – hooray, whoopee, phew!

I outline my case; she says, "Are you sure?"
Oh no, was my joy to be premature?
"Scout's honour," I say; she still harbours doubts,
Demanding to know my bin's whereabouts.

"Was it left in the street?" "Yes, it was, on my life!
I swear I'm not trying to cause any strife!"
"Calm down, just calm down: the day, was it right?"
"It was – 'twas this morning; please, please expedite;

"I *am* well prepared for every collection!"
"This is what *you* say; but your recollection…"
"My recol— I beg you, just empty the bin!"
This being the point my head starts to spin;

But worse is to come – another retort:
"But our contractors, they didn't report…"
"*Of course*, they did not: they missed it, all right?
It's hot: it will rot and may cause a blight."

"All right, I will tell them." A headway at last?
"They'll come back today?" She now sounds aghast:
"*Today*? No, no, no, that's *not* how it works."
"So *how* does it work, then?" (I want to shout, "Jerks!")

"It's forty-eight hours; this is what it'll take."
"Please, please, just make sure…" (My calmness is fake.)
Two days have now passed – my bin is still there;
Its contents do stink, and I'm going spare;

I thus call the council, and they let me know
My call is important but queueing is slow;
They keep me on hold; I have sweaty palms:
They play horrid tunes – I wish it were Brahms…

But never mind the horrid tunes: guys, please come back. All is forgiven and forgotten, and I will never complain about a missed bin *ever* again.

Wait, wait, I've just realised another huge omission on my part: we are more than half-way through the proceedings, and I haven't yet told you that Keswick is the most dog-friendly place in the whole universe, I mean country. It's so sweet! I'm also a dog lover (in fact, I'm an animal lover), so the thought that the lovely natives and I have at least one thing *genuinely* in common is most heartening.

> Once in England, one discovers
> It's a nation of dog lovers,
> Whose endorphins get a boost
> As their pooches rule the roost.

> Here is Buster, a Great Dane
> Bounding briskly down the lane
> Hauling Mrs Smith, his slave;
> Gosh, this lady must be brave.

> Fluffy Dixie, the Maltese,
> Can be handled with some ease,
> But her vassal must ensure
> Her twice-weekly pawdicure.

> Connoisseur Welsh Terrier Wyatt
> Has a very special diet,
> Fresh, organic; his Miss Grove
> Labours hours by the stove.

And this German Shepherd, Giles,
Walks his servant thirty miles;
All these walkies make them fit
(Pity 'bout the 'German' bit.)

Mrs Johnson's Pug called Nino
Loves his frothy puppucino
Made with most delicious cream –
She would serve it, and he'd beam.

Playful Buddy likes a puddle,
Then he races for his cuddle
And, oblivious to the glower,
Gives his John a muddy shower,

Whereas Bella drags her ma
To her weekly doggy spa,
Place that says: "We beautify
With brush-out and fluff blow-dry."

One's enslavement is no surprise:
Those waggly tails, these puppy eyes,
And one can hardly catch one's breath
When one is licked (*ouch!*) half to death.

Though it's all charming, I must end
My paean to the man's best friend
With this appeal: Dear owners, please
Don't hang the poo bags on the trees!

13

The Red Brexit Bus, More of My Lakeland Adventures and My Knackered Hip

If I had known that I would have had to wait for a new hip for five years, I wouldn't have knackered my old one. But they had promised to give the NHS an extra £350 million a week, hadn't they? On the side of the big red bus. You remember this big red bus, don't you? You couldn't help but fall for its solemn pledge of this incredible Brexit bonus in those heady days when Britain was making its audacious bid for freedom. Well, they do say that hindsight is a wonderful thing…

> Some years back they decked out this red bus,
> Which, they thought, would not cause any fuss;
> But its promise of mountains of dosh
> Did turn out a big ruse and much tosh.

> NHS, they would say, will – yes! – thrive,
> With this dough (much of it) and our drive;
> Yet, despite such a claim (which is bold),
> Don't fall ill, break your hip or grow old.

So, oblivious to the worsening state of our beleaguered NHS, with which I'd had very limited contact hitherto, I did knacker my hip. Easily done when you are a Lakeland afficionado. If you'd like some tips on how to achieve this – after all, you might fancy a shiny new hip yourself – they are coming right up.

I've already told you that one of the places I couldn't easily get to under my own steam was Wasdale. And ensconced in Wasdale was the magnificent Yewbarrow. By no means the highest, the plucky fell nevertheless held its own, being defended by formidable scrambles at both ends and by precipitous slopes on both sides. I had climbed it already but was nearing the end of my next round of all the Wainwright fells and was determined to bag it again. In fact, the closer to the end of each round I got, the fiercer the drive to complete it became. Actually, this reminded me of George Mallory: on his final attempt to conquer Everest, he felt that it was either him or the mountain: a fight to the death. No, no, I'm not for a moment comparing myself to him; I'm simply trying to say that I think I understand how he must have felt. So I was going to bag Yewbarrow come hell or high water.

So, again, I summon Garry with the taxicab, and he drops me off at the foot of the fell's southern ridge, culminating on the towering pinnacle of Bell Rib, and abandons me there. Miles away from any transport which

I could use for return, I begin my climb. The bracken-clad ridge is steep but easy, and my progress is swift. I reach the very craggy section at the top and follow a thin track leading straight up a narrow gully. The gully steepens with every step, but, high above me, I can see a rocky cleft delineated against the sky. The going should get easier on the other side, I tell myself. Slowly, I negotiate the steep scree and finally reach the cleft. Oops! On the other side, there is a sheer drop of several hundred feet plunging right down to Wast Water glistening right at the bottom of the valley. I'm trapped. Why, oh why hadn't I re-read the Wainwright guide? The famous author clearly warns that Bell Rib is 'a bad trap for the unwary walker'. And I'm now getting punished for my complacency.

The thing about steep gullies is that they are much easier going up than the other way. I turn around and wonder how on earth I'm going to get myself back down. In fact, I'm terrified. If I hadn't already had one mountain rescue under my belt, I would have called 999, but I couldn't bring myself to inconvenience those wonderful guys and gals again. So, using my rear end as well as my hands and feet (in specialist climbing circles, this descent technique is known as 'five points of contact'), I inch myself down very slowly until, finally, I reach easier ground. If I'd had transport waiting for me at the bottom, I would have abandoned my climb, but I didn't, so, though shaken, I felt that I had to press on.

Although I still had scrambles to contend with – the ones I should have headed for in the first place but inexplicably missed – they were easier, and I experienced the usual thrill on reaching Great Door: you go from seeing only the slope you are scrambling up to a sudden, magnificent, vista of the lofty Scafell range opposite. The long summit ridge then pleasantly conveyed me to the top, from which, by now, I had trialled my own, largely grassy, escape route to the bottom of the Overbeck Valley: nothing would have induced me to descend by the formidable Stirrup Crag scrambles, which I had earlier found to be much more challenging than those on Yewbarrow's south side. On reaching Dore Head, forming the northern brim of the valley, I briefly enjoyed the magnificent view of the high fells fringing Mosedale, the mighty Pillar and Kirk Fell being the most prominent, but I needed to get myself down to Wasdale Head as quickly as I could, having wasted much time getting stuck up Bell Rib. The descent from Dore Head was not only very steep but made uncomfortable by loose scree, but I reached Wasdale Head in one piece. Alas, no comfy car was waiting for me there, so I then had to climb out of the valley, my escape route leading over Sty Head, the pass I've already mentioned, carved between the massive slopes of Great Gable and Great End – an appropriate appellation in each case. The final four miles, down into Borrowdale and all the way to the bus stop in Seatoller, were well-rehearsed and passed fairly quickly: it must have been all that Yewbarrow adrenaline still coursing through my veins.

But there were many more, longer and more strenuous, hikes. Take, for example, this linear walk from Ennerdale Bridge to Seatoller via Honister Pass, made possible by one of these ephemeral Sunday buses of the early noughties, now as dead as a dodo. It was eighteen miles of unremitting ups and downs: Crag Fell, Ennerdale

Fell, Caw Fell, Haycock, Great Scoat Fell, Little Scoat Fell, Pillar and then all the way to Honister Pass along Kirk Fell Terrace and Moses Trod. And guess what happened on Honister Pass: yep, the last bus had gone, so I had to sprint down to Seatoller, hoping for better luck there. On that occasion, Lady Luck did smile on me, but I wouldn't recommend sprinting after such a strenuous hike. Unless you are a marathon runner.

Or this epic hike, which partially overlapped with the previous one but which, at twenty-one miles, was even longer and more strenuous and which tested my endurance to the limit. Starting at Seatoller, I hiked all the way to Ennerdale Bridge, but, on this occasion, over Sty Head, Middle Fell, Haycock, Caw Fell, Ennerdale Fell and Crag Fell, with the painful but unavoidable transit along the bottom of Wasdale. The original plan was to catch the return bus at Ennerdale Bridge, but the huge distance, coupled with several thousand feet of ascent, made this impossible, so this was another Garry job. Come to think of it, the man should be able to retire in his prime, what with all the fares he has collected from me over the years.

Or take this sixteen-miler with a considerable off-piste section. To climb Whin Rigg, Illgill Head, Slight Side and Scafell, I needed to get myself to Nether Wasdale, so Garry with his taxicab was again pressed into service – not even a most ephemeral of buses would stray there. And it was a long drive, so the lift certainly wasn't cheap. But it was my name-day present to myself. You know about name days, don't you? You don't? Name days are huge in Poland – much bigger than birthdays. We often name our kids after saints, and each saint has his or her own day in the calendar. All Poles thus know that St Anna's day falls on 26 July, which is the date of my name day. So there can be no excuse not to get the Annas they know a lovely name-day card. And a bunch of flowers. You can't say that we are not superior in this respect, each of us owning two special days per year and thus legitimately expecting a double helping of cards and presents. In Britain, only the late Queen used to enjoy such a privilege.

> You do know just where you stand
> With this very Polish brand
> Designated as name day;
> I'll explain this right away.
>
> We have all these saints, so we
> Give our kids their names, you see.
> Anna, Mary, Peter, Joan –
> All are very widely known;
>
> Each has its calendar date,
> Which is when we celebrate –
> Easy to identify;
> Anna's name day? In July.
>
> But in Britain, it's quite fraught;
> Names do give you food for thought,
> Many being really quaint:
> Does Boo-Bliss have her own saint?
>
> Chardonnay? It does sound fine,
> But I thought that it was wine.

> Deklyn, Karleb, Casey-Jay:
> I am sure they are OK,
> But they seem a British quirk;
> Name days here just wouldn't work.

Back in Nether Wasdale, I bid Garry a slightly teary farewell (I haven't booked him for the return journey because I have no idea when my escapade might end) and tackle the steep ascent of Whin Rigg by scrambling straight up one of its formidable gullies. Unlike its nearby counterparts, this one is climbable, conveying me to the magnificent ridge leading to Illgill Head and separating Wasdale from Miterdale. Having descended to Burnmoor Tarn, I am faced with the vast pathless western slope of Slight Side, this fell being my next goal. Although the map shows no routes leading to the top from this side, I have no option but to plough on, so I stagger up, trying my best not to fall into any of the holes concealed by the tussocky grass. From the attractive craggy summit, a sky-scraping ridge conveys me to the rocky top of Scafell, a fantastic viewpoint with a 360-degree panorama taking in all the Lakeland's greats, prominent among them being the neighbouring Scafell Pike, with its mandatory hundreds of pilgrims swarming on the top, Ill Crag, Esk Pike, Bowfell and Crinkle Crags. The route then leads steeply down by Foxes Tarn, below which I'm having to negotiate a stony gully which gets hardly any sun and is thus gloomy and damp. But that's not the end of the descent because I have to get right to the bottom of Upper Eskdale – only to have to climb back up to Esk Hause, now appearing higher than its 2,500 feet. Throughout the descent, the rugged mountain scenery is awe-inspiring, but, as I finally stand on Esk Hause, I'm beginning to flag. The final descent of the day takes me along Grains Gill to Stockley Bridge before the last, painful, two-and-a-half miles to Seatoller. It's evening already, and the last bus to Keswick has gone. I thus call Garry to taxi me home. He did quite well out of me on my name day.

Talking of Scafell Pike and Scafell, I now find it hard to believe that there was a time when climbing the former from Seatoller simply wasn't enough. I remember getting to the summit for twelve noon and sitting there wondering how the heck I was going to fill the rest of the day: twelve miles and 3,000 feet of ascent simply weren't going to cut it. So the next logical thing seemed to be to continue to Scafell, although both mountains are separated by a deep depression. Wainwright thus asserted that 'medals have been won for lesser deeds' – meaning climbing both fells during the same hike. But, hey, I was still on the right side of fifty (although only just) so handled the Foxes Tarn route with gusto, emerging on the much quieter summit without feeling particularly fatigued. With no transport, I couldn't descend to Wasdale and, instead, needed to head back to Seatoller. I thus used the incredibly steep, but sheltered, Lord's Rake, down which I simply slid on my posterior. The rake never sees the sun, which is why its stones are usually wet, so you can imagine the state of the seat of my climbing pants. But I wasn't competing in the Miss Pristine competition, was I? From the bottom of the rake, I followed a narrow path hugging the base of the ferocious crags forming Scafell's buttresses. This trail led me to Mickledore, overtopped by the notorious Broad

Stand, which, infuriatingly, blocks the direct passage between Scafell Pike and Scafell. From there, I climbed the Pike again, as you do. And, after descending to Lingmell Col, I still had enough sap to scale Lingmell before descending along the Corridor Route and over Sty Head.

Another unquestionable contributor to the knackering of my hip was my Central Ridge escapade. The Central Ridge runs all the way from the famous Langdale Pikes to Bleaberry Fell, where it tapers down virtually to Keswick. Well, at least I wouldn't need any transport back. So I call Garry again: although I could have got myself to Great Langdale with the aid of two buses, I had an inkling that a very early start was in order. I climb the angular Harrison Stickle, the highest of the five magnificent Pikes, via the unfrequented Pike Howe route. It never ceases to amaze me that the route seems to have escaped the attention of the throng who invariably climbs to Stickle Tarn along the Stickle Ghyll path. Well, their loss, my gain: let nobody tell you that you can't escape crowds in the Lake District – you can, easily. That said, the summit of Harrison Stickle is crowded – it usually is. From there, there is an easy passage to another Pike, Thunacar Knott, which looks nothing like a pike. A wide ridge then gently rises to High Raise before descending to Greenup Edge, a well-known thoroughfare between Borrowdale and Grasmere.

The subsequent ascent of Ullscarf, considered by some to be sitting close to the geographical centre of the Lake District fells, is squelchy in places, but the view from the summit offers ample compensation for the wet boots. In fact, the views are spectacular throughout the entire walk, the Central Ridge forming a high spine running through the middle of Lakeland – partially in parallel with the even loftier Helvellyn ridge. It is after I descend past the dramatic Standing Crag that my Golgotha starts: from where the Watendlath path crosses mine, the Central Ridge is abominably wet, and, by the time I reach the slight elevation of High Tove, my boots are thoroughly soaked. But much worse is to come: nobody has told me about the detestable peat hags between this summit and High Seat (this was still in my pre-Wainwright days). Recently (I mean from the perspective of 2023), this section has been transformed out of all recognition, with the new passage skilfully engineered out of large slabs being a delight to walk along. This fantastic work has been carried out by an equally fantastic conservation partnership called Fix the Fells. And you know who funded the project? I'm not entirely sure if it's safe to utter their name, but it was the European Regional Development Fund (ERDF). Until those European imperialists wrapped their tentacles around Lakeland, you could tackle this horrendously muddy bit only during a drought or freeze – unless you were a masochist. Admittedly, Vinnie does think that, when it comes to mountains, I'm not entirely compos mentis, but at least most of my lunacies became lunacies only in retrospect.

I am thus cursing under my breath as I am trying to pull each leg out of the awful mud trying to swallow me whole. I am exhausted by the time I reach the summit of High Seat, and there is still more wetness to contend with during my passage to Bleaberry Fell, the last mountain in the Central Ridge. I then somehow manage to stagger across the sprawling Low Moss at the back of Walla Crag, a delightful fell which, thankfully, is now less than an hour away from my house. In urgent need of a pick-me-up, I'm trying to remind myself of how strong women are; after all, we have two X chromosomes – unlike men.

> Women are the weaker sex?
> But we've got this X *plus* X!
> It's a brilliant chromosome,
> Whose importance did hit home
>
> When I learnt how much it means
> To have all these lovely genes
> Helping us to be immune
> From diseases – what a boon!
>
> X is where they all reside,
> And this fills me with great pride,
> For we have a double dose;
> Blokes may well be bellicose
>
> Owing to their manly Y,
> Which determines every guy,
> But we do get more protection
> From contagion and infection.
>
> We might have a gentler streak,
> But who says that we are weak?
> Misconception so abysmal:
> Our strength is organismal!

Buoyed up by the reminder of my organismal strength, I finally reach home. Although I never again attempted the Central Ridge in its entirety, my adventures continued unabated. Take, for example, another ridge hike which was, for a long time, the summer staple for Bobby, Patti and me and which we used to do at least once a year. You got the bus to the top of Kirkstone Pass and then walked all the way to Pooley Bridge over Cauldale Moor, Thornthwaite Crag, High Street, Rampsgill Head, High Raise, Raven Howe, Wether Hill, Loadpot Hill and Arthur's Pike, descending to Pooley Bridge past the ancient Cockpit. Some fourteen miles of an unadulterated delight, save for the scramble on the descent from Cauldale Moor to Threshthwaite Mouth. Apparently, much of the ridge had been used by the Romans as a high-level passage between two forts: one in Ambleside and one near Penrith, so we were treading in history's footsteps. In fact, the loftiest mountain in the ridge, High Street, has been named after this Roman road. See what fabulous walks you could do by using buses. And, to a large extent, you still can.

Then there was the hike from Ings to Patterdale via Kentmere and over Shipman Knotts, Kentmere Pike, Harter Fell (Mardale), Nan Bield Pass, Mardale Ill Bell and High Street and then past Angle Tarn and down from Boredale Hause to Patterdale. What was particularly memorable about that day was the extreme heat: I had the mountains virtually to myself, other walkers having sensibly heeded the warnings, repeatedly issued on the radio and TV, to stay in the shade and to avoid all exertions. But, of course, these warnings did not apply to me, did they? Given the exceptional conditions, this adventure has undoubtedly eclipsed my several repeats of the thirteen-mile long Kentmere Horseshoe, which seemed tame in comparison. And, in case you were wondering if I had managed to tackle the horseshoe while getting to Kentmere by public transport, the answer is yes. Years ago, Friends of the Lake District sponsored another ephemeral bus, which ran from Kendal to Kentmere. But, travelling on an early bus from Keswick, I was able to intercept it at Staveley. Seems incredible now. But even more incredible is how I managed to complete the entire round and still catch the return bus. Yet I always did, although not without a mad dash at the end.

Another hike which springs to mind was that from Great Langdale to Coniston over Crinkle Crags. My friend Julian and I reached the fell after an adventurous full-frontal assault, whereupon we proceeded to Little Stand (which isn't little at all), with a descent all the way to Cockley Beck. Lunch was consumed on the go as we sped along the bottom of the remote Duddon Valley (that of my Green Crag and Harter Fell adventures) because I knew that, if we were to stand any chance of catching the last bus from Coniston, we couldn't afford any stops. Very much like Vinnie and me on our infamous twenty-one-mile three-valley hike. And as we were trying to give ourselves indigestion, we were readying ourselves for the climb to Seathwaite Reservoir, followed by a further ascent to Goat's Hause, sitting high up between Coniston Old Man and Dow Crag. The descent took us past Goat's Water to Walna Scar Road, which in turn conveyed us all the way down to Coniston – with two minutes to spare before the last bus to Ambleside! For a long time afterwards, Julian kept marvelling at how I had managed to time the hike with such precision, and it pained me to admit that it had happened more by accident than by design.

And by no means were such hikes one-offs. Since, however, this book strives to strike a balance between my mountain escapades, jocular musings and satirical asides, I had better stop here. Admittedly, I have managed to capture only a fraction of my Lakeland adventures – after all, I've had a quarter of a century to pack them into – but I imagine it is enough to make you appreciate that, in the end, something had to give out. And what gave out first was my hip.

> My hip, I have told you, is on the way out,
> I need a new one, of this there's no doubt;
> Thank goodness we have our dear NHS,
> Heroic, lifesaving – despite all the stress.
>
> An X-ray confirms that things do look grim,
> Arthritis afflicting my tired old limb,
> I'm sent to an expert: he does hips and knees;
> To him, I am sure, it will be a breeze.
>
> Consultant they call him – he must be so smart;
> I try to spruce up, and then I depart.
> The hospital's busy, so I have to wait,
> They say he is sorry that he's running late.

At long last, they call me: I knock on the door,
He answers, "Come in." I do – and am done for:
His features: so chiselled, so manly, so fine –
A dart of delight shoots right down my spine.

He says, "Please lie down," gets up from his stool:
He is six foot five! I wobble and drool.
"It's strange," he announces and shifts on the spot,
"The wobble's a symptom – the drooling is not.

"Grab hold of you knee, pull it up to your chin;"
The shape of his earlobe – I'm pining within,
My chest overflowing with longing and ache,
But all I can do is lie there and shake.

He scratches his head, "Now, this is most odd:
These shakes, that's quite new," then gives a grave nod.
The mole on his chin! Exquisite? You bet!
So all I can do is redden and sweat.

"Rosacea and sweating: *The Lancet*, I think:
I might have discovered some strange causal link."
He scribbles some notes, I look at his lips;
The fateful conclusion: I need two new hips.

"That's all, we are done." This shatters my trance;
I make for the door with one final glance,
His profile a sight that I cannot efface;
He murmurs, "Strange symptoms – groundbreaking, this case…"

Dear Dr I.C., my Wonderful Consultant Orthopaedic Surgeon, I sincerely hope that you will forgive my poetic licence – not that one can accuse my doggerel of approximating poetry. But that's all I can manage. Anyway, I will be forever grateful to you for freeing me from excruciating pain and for giving me my life back – literally. Since my readers (if there are any, that is) are unfamiliar with the story, I'm duty-bound to stress that it wasn't you who had kept me in pain for five years. Quite the opposite! You acted with lightning speed, operating on me within one month – *one month!* – of my desperate self-referral, honouring the five years I had been allowed to suffer under a different consultant at another hospital. You embody the very best of the NHS, and my indebtedness will stalk you to the ends of the Earth. Thanks to you, I continue to have fabulous adventures in our spell-binding Lake District and have been able to write this book, although whether the latter can be seen as a plus is undoubtedly open to dispute. But I'm trying to take good care of the fantastic new hip you have given me: no more twenty-milers for me. Thank you from the bottom of my heart!

14

FOMO, FBI and Skiddaw u3a

What a colossal oversight: I haven't told you about my lovely Roamers yet. Actually, it's not entirely true: I've mentioned them a couple of times already, but you are about to get acquainted with them properly. The Roamers are a fabulous walking group led by me. No, they are not fabulous because they are led by me – they are fabulous because of their own innate fabulousness. I will introduce them to you in the next chapter. But, first, I have to tell you about how I discovered people. It happened in 2015. Until then, I had been largely solitary, walking by myself for most of the time. Admittedly, when I became friends with Bobby and Patti, I did hike with them as well. After all, they were (Bobby still is, and Patti is charming the pants off all the angels in Heaven) both so lovely that you couldn't not want to be around them. But, essentially, I remained a lone wolf, and the mere prospect of joining anything would bring me out in a rash.

I could thus never understand the idea behind FOMO: Fear of Missing Out. If you are not included in things, you can stay at home and read all those fascinating books on English grammar rather than going to stupid parties where you don't know anybody and have to make idiotic small talk and where somebody inadvertently spills red wine down your cleavage. Actually, it was the guy whose interest in that part of your anatomy was perhaps a little too keen. So I am much more of an FBI person myself. No, no, no, no, no (I'm sure you can detect Michael Gove's influence here): I don't mean the Federal Bureau of Investigation at all. Just read this verse, please.

> Fear of Missing Out –
> What's all *that* about?
> Mine is not a sin:
> Fear of Being In.

Yep, my Fear of Being In had kept me out of all clubs, associations, societies, unions, congregations, assemblies, caucuses, partnerships, fraternities, bands, clans, communities, cabals, coteries and, generally, groupings of any kind. For a long, long time. Then, suddenly, I am walloped by a rather disconcerting thought: there will be nobody at my funeral. I mean, I don't expect a crowd, obviously, but three people would be nice. And I can't get this pesky thought out of my head. After all, I'm not getting any younger, you know.

Still, I can't bring myself to join anything, and it's only a serendipitous occurrence that changes the course of my life. I devise another one of my schemes, as one does, and Patti, good-naturedly, agrees to go along with it. The scheme involves climbing Harter Fell from the top of Hardknott Pass, to which we can't get under our own steam (Patti doesn't drive either). Although Garry with his taxicab has started giving me a discount – I am a regular, after all – a taxi ride would still be expensive (as you know, Harter Fell is far away), so I call our Voluntary Car Scheme. You know about Voluntary Car Scheme, don't you? You don't? No, you wouldn't: you are a motorist. This fantastic scheme has been devised for people who either don't or can't drive and charges less than a taxi. It's mostly used for doctors' appointments and hospital trips, but its remit extends to outings with friends: I have checked. You don't think I would do anything untoward, surely? After all, if I did, you might deport me. And the bike guy would be rubbing his hands with glee.

So I call those good people, and, a few days later, this car pulls up in front of my house. It's driven by this very tall and handsome guy (we could see that he was very tall when he got out to open the car door for us; what a gent). And, as we travel, we start chatting. Suddenly, he turns to me and says, "You are not a nun, are you?" *A nun?* Goodness gracious, no! Apparently, his despatcher had told him I was a nun – no idea why. OK, I may look slightly saintly, but I didn't know I sounded saintly too.

That said, if you only knew what I used to get up to in my younger days! But you don't. And you won't. Because I won't tell you. In those pre-social media days, nothing was recorded, and all my youthful blunders and misdeeds were shielded from public gaze. Anyway, they were all committed abroad (I mean your abroad – not mine).

In this day and age, can you imagine the blissfulness of obscurity and anonymity? You try Googling me, and you won't find anything on me. Nowt, zilch, diddly-squat. I mean anything compromising; you will definitely find the info on my books there. But I'm prepared to admit to a small misdemeanour. Just don't tell the guy on the bike.

> OK, I smoked weed but didn't inhale;
> After all, looking cool was our Holy Grail;
> In our blithe youth,
> We all smoked, in truth:
> It did go quite well with cheapie light ale.

I'm in good company, though: after all, Boris Johnson, Michel Gove, Dominic Raab and the like have openly admitted to having dabbled in drugs in their younger days, and it didn't do them any harm. And, even more seriously, if Theresa May could run through a field of wheat and still get elected prime minister...

Anyway, we chat away, and he tells us that he leads a local walking group. They are called the Roamers and operate under the auspices of Skiddaw u3a. By the time he delivers us to the top of Hardknott Pass, we have become friends. In fact, I think he is so nice that I decide to join his walking group. So I do. Wonders never cease! That's when I discover people properly. What a revelation! The folk in the group are delightful. As is Chris, the very tall and handsome guy who drove us to Hardknott Pass and who had founded the group (tragically, no longer with us). He also leads many of the walks. Although, in the Lake District, I don't need a guide, I join many of the walks simply because the company is so lovely. And when Chris is away, I even lead several walks for him. And then, what does he go and do? Moves to Scotland. The group is thus in danger of becoming rudderless. Who is going to replace him? After some deliberation, I put my name forward. After all, in the aftermath of the Brexit vote I need as many feathers in my cap as I can muster. I get selected. Admittedly, from the shortlist of one, but it's an honour nevertheless.

Now, what do I do? I have never been at the helm of anything in my life. Or led anybody (apart from the few instances when I was deputising for Chris). OK, I might have attempted to guide Bobby, but, when I did, I got him lost. Perhaps this little verse will relieve my tension.

> Founding Roamers was astute –
> Move we all, as one, salute;
> Chris was ably at the helm,
> And the Lakeland was his realm;
> There were splendid walks galore,
> Lovely friendships by the score,
>
> Laughter, frolics, fun, mirth, joy
> And those leg-pulls – boy, oh boy!
> His departure, keenly felt,
> Was a blow so fiercely dealt,
> And the void he left so deep
> That one couldn't help but weep;
>
> Now it's me with whom you're stuck,
> (It is truly rotten luck);
> I am trying (some say very),

But it's still all rather scary;
One needs Chris's gift and skill,
For his boots are *huge* to fill!

So that's how I became a walk leader – albeit voluntary, but you can't have everything. I'm dying to introduce you to some of my lovely Roamers, but I can't do this until I explain that I am not just any old walk leader, oh no. My group is a part of Skiddaw u3a, which is, in turn, a part of the u3a. I think I have already mentioned the University of the Third Age, haven't I? It's a fantastic international movement for people who have entered their third – vintage – age. Think about it: the kids have flown the nest, you have either retired or reduced your work hours and you are still in good working order, bar the odd artificial hip or knee (or both), colostomy bag, hearing aid, pacemaker and set of brand-new dentures. So you are bursting with all this health and, finally, you have the chance to do what you have always wanted to do but never got round to doing. *And* you've got your free bus pass – yippee! That's precisely where the wonderful u3a comes in.

u3a: we all, as one,
Learn, laugh, live and have much fun,
Celebrating our age,
With new projects centre stage;

Now's the time to fix our gaze
On the next, exciting, phase
Of our journey, in which we,
Unimpeded, joyous, free,

Will share know-how, learn new things,
Make good friends and spread our wings,
With the brilliant u3a
Right behind us all the way.

All are welcome though its door,
Every passion's catered for,
Every skill is in demand,
No one's churlish or off-hand.

Always wanted to learn French
Or know how to use a wrench?
You'll be welcome at a class,
But there's no exam to pass.

Music, gardening, GPS,
Archaeology and chess,
Are all offered (so much choice
Is a reason to rejoice),

So are writing, film and art,
Which will gratify you heart;
Bridge will exercise your mind,
Books will help you to unwind,

Whereas dancing will, for sure,
Draw you in with its allure;
There is walking, dining out:
Groups you wouldn't be without,

> Not to mention racquetball,
> Or researching urban sprawl,
> Although these are but a few
> Among those laid on for you.

> If you haven't joined us yet,
> Worry not and do not fret:
> Find your local u3a,
> And enrol without delay!

And my local u3a is Skiddaw u3a, which caters for Keswick and the surrounding area. Just think of it: I am a part of it! So, I take my leadership duties extremely seriously. And you can't be a good leader without being upfront with your charges. Although, as always, you try to distance yourself a little from the subject by using the third person.

> She has relished and savoured her role,
> Leading Roamers has made her feel whole;
> But you take a big gamble
> When you go on her ramble:
> The thing is, you see, she's a Pole.

I do, however, try to compensate for this deficiency. Very hard. You see, when I walk by myself, I concentrate on the route. But when I lead my lovely Roamers, I concentrate on trying to shine, sparkle and scintillate (I told you I was good at tautology). And scintillation is where I must end this chapter. Because it's best to finish on a positive note. After all, the next chapter will be about my fall from grace.

But I will also introduce you properly to my wonderful group – at long last.

Hold on, hold on, I've just realised that, apart from the freedom to join the u3a, I haven't pointed out other delights of our vintage age – and they are considerable.

> You might have a dodgy knee,
> But you're overcome with glee:
> In your vintage age,
> You've become a sage,
> And you do get your flu jab for free!

And there are even more compensations when you get to seventy, you know.

> When you're sixty-five, then you
> Get the jab that conquers flu,
> There is also (did they warn ya?)
> Jab that helps you fight pneumonia;
>
> But when you're three score and ten,
> You are in the state of zen
> 'Cos (this vision gives me tingles)
> You will get the jab for shingles!

Well, the jab is actually *against* shingles, but you get my drift. So don't forget to ask for yours when you get to seventy. I had meant to make mine the centrepiece of my seventieth birthday last year, but a walk with my lovely Roamers got in the way – inexplicably. But that's definitely where I'm stopping for now: the next chapter is just over the page.

15

Mishaps on the Fells and My Lovely Roamers

I've just confessed that, when I lead a walk, I concentrate on trying to shine, sparkle and scintillate. Not sure why. Maybe, after my being a hermit for decades, my long-supressed innate exuberance, ebullience and effervescence have suddenly decided to erupt. A bit like the pus being released from a lanced boil.

Now, finally, is the time to take you back to Seat Sandal, where Bobby and I ended up after my Easter poppy seed cake feast. I had told him about this gentle descent which we could use in future if it met with his approval. Another reason why I had dragged him up there was that I wanted to exorcise a painful recent memory. I think I've already said this much.

Which swiftly brings me to said memory. I greatly relish introducing my lovely Roamers to new routes. And quite a few of my charges hadn't climbed Seat Sadal. Aha, here was my opportunity to show off – I mean to shine. I have to tell you that I am usually extremely modest, but when one has amassed such extraordinary knowledge of the Lake District and has such amazing navigational and organisational skills, one finds it rather hard to hide one's light under a bushel. I had advertised the walk as having this very pleasant descent down the gentle shoulder leading all the way to The Traveller's Rest near Grasmere. The route wasn't marked on the *Ordnance Survey* map, but the group were fortunate in having this marvellous guide who was going to offer them a most rewarding experience. Just to make sure that this point wasn't lost on anybody (I like making sure), I kept waxing lyrical about the delights of the aforementioned shoulder.

The day had an excellent start: we got off the bus at the end of Armboth Road near the southern tip of Thirlmere and struck south along the bottom of the steep Birk Side, riven by the gully of the foaming Birkside Gill – always a captivating sight. True, the crossing of Rise Beck, flowing out of Grisedale Tarn higher up, was rather tricky, this marvellous guide having forgotten that there was no bridge there. Oops! But our indomitable gents rose to the occasion, valiantly helping the ladies to negotiate the slippery stones without ending up in the tumbling beck. Thanks to them, we all made it to the other side and could now commence our ascent along the aforementioned other side of Rise Beck.

As we went up the rough path steeply tracing the cascading stream, the descending mist was beginning to thicken. When we emerged at the top of the beck, from where we should have been able to see the nearby Grisedale Tarn, there was nothing to discern. We immersed ourselves in the dark thick soup, I navigating our ascent of Seat Sandal with the help of an old wall, which, I remembered, should be kept to our right throughout. Finally, we could see no higher ground anywhere around and realised that we had reached the summit of Seat Sandal. Now was the opportunity for me to display my superb navigational skills. In case anybody's spirit was in need of being buoyed up, however, I repeated the 'you will love this shoulder' refrain, confidently turning onto the path which, I believed, would deliver us to the top of my planned descent route. So confident was I that I was even teasing my companions, asking them for a quiet prayer that we wouldn't end up in Patterdale, which lay in exactly the opposite direction and from which we wouldn't have been able to extricate ourselves without making a considerable bus detour via Penrith. So we waded through the thick mist merrily, with me, now rather nauseatingly, enquiring if my companions were enjoying this lovely route.

But wait – why is this path getting steeper? It wasn't meant to! Suddenly, my heart sinks and adrenaline start pumping: I had clearly missed the turn-off for this easy shoulder, and we were now following the wrong path. As we continued descending, the trail steepening with every step, the mist started lifting and my worst fears were confirmed: straight ahead loomed the steep slope of Steel Fell plunging down to the top of Dunmail Raise – nowhere near Grasmere's Traveller's Rest, where we were supposed to have ended up. There was now nothing for it but to put on a brave face, and I kept promising the group that the now very steep descent would soon be over. It was – *eventually* – although several posteriors had to be engaged in our downward slide. I've already explained that this particular descent technique is known as 'five points of contact'. Sadly, two brand-new Roamers, a lovely couple, were so bruised by the experience that they never showed up again. Serves me right! But this mishap at least gave me the excuse to write this limerick.

> "One knows one's route," she'll smugly say,
> "My knowledge *always* saves the day."
> They all nod, her friends,
> Thick mist then descends,
> At which point, she loses the way.

But I didn't need the assistance of thick mist to go wrong. Two years previously, on a blazingly hot summer's day, I set off to lead my lovely Roamers up Arnison Crags and Birks in the Eastern Fells, a route unfamiliar to some of them. Now was the time to gently remind everyone of my impressive local knowledge. I just couldn't help myself, could I? The route from Patterdale to Arnison Crags was straightforward enough, simply following a wall up the brackeny slope. We then had a delightful time sunning ourselves on the pretty rocky summit and admiring the breathtaking vista. But it was the passage to Birks that was to be my pièce de résistance. Not marked on the OS map, the route follows a faint trail, one of several criss-crossing the area. These trails meander their way pleasantly among grassy knolls dotting the sprawling plateau above Glenamara Park and can be a tad confusing, but, hey, my lovely Roamers had me to guide them. The key was to avoid the direct steep ascent of Birks, and I knew exactly how to perform this manoeuvre. There then followed several further reminders of the superiority of 'my', supposedly secret, passage, which avoided all the steepness. Instead, the trail would lead us gently up across the grassy slope towards the depression between St Sunday Crag and Birks, from where a similarly gentle ridge would convey us straight to the latter's summit.

So why did the path suddenly start getting steeper? When I realised that I had missed the correct, albeit rather indistinct, turn-off, we were already committed to the steep direct ascent along the wall above Trough Head. What's more, the day was stiflingly hot, the unremitting steepness making matters worse, and I could only apologise profusely. But, as always, my lovely Roamers were very understanding, refraining from grumbling, moaning and whining (I believe that, in similar circumstances, tautology is entirely justifiable) while, at the same time, pulling my leg ever so gently. (When I first came to this country, I kept imploring the lovely natives to stop pulling my *legs*, but my walking companions are kinder, always limiting themselves to pulling at one only.) In fact, it is everybody's sense of humour (alongside their other remarkable attributes) that makes our walks an utter delight.

But I don't always come clean. On a walk starting – and terminating – in the charming village of Caldbeck on a rainy day in the middle of a wet spell – or was it a very wet spell? – we reached Nether Row and needed to return to the village. We thus start descending along what advertises itself as a footpath: after all, there is a footpath sign at its entry. But it is more akin to a groove, which has now become a fast-flowing stream. The faux footpath is hemmed in by two prickly hedges, so there is no way of avoiding the water. We thus wade downstream, our boots getting a thorough soaking in the process; there is no footwear that would have withstood this onslaught.

What's worse, Parson's Park, rising above Caldbeck, which I am using for visual navigation (yes, I know, I know, I should have learnt how to use a compass), has, inexplicably, moved to the left, which is when I realise I have gone wrong. Has the group also twigged? I glance at my companions, but it looks as if everyone is too focused on trying to keep upright to bother surveying their surroundings; besides, they are being led by an experienced and knowledgeable mountain guide, aren't they? Adrenaline pumping, I know we have to veer left at the earliest opportunity, which thankfully presents itself at the bottom of the groove. Relief! What's more, a signpost for Caldbeck confirms that, finally, I am on the right track. We reach the village thoroughly soaked but without further mishaps, with me keeping shtum that the intended route would have involved no more than an easy descent along a minor tarmac road. But nobody asked, so, while tempted to confess, I didn't. Politicians would undoubtedly call this an innocent non-disclosure of inconsequential intelligence.

The picture of my new-discovered companionability wouldn't, however, be complete if I didn't mention that I also joined Keswick Rambling Club (KRC) and have led some of its walks. One of them would take us up two medium-height Wainwright fells: Sallows and Sour Howes, standing guard above Windermere's Troutbeck. Unfortunately, it was one of those annoying days when a cloud inversion allows high mountains to bask in sunshine while swathing lower terrain in fog. Our ascent along the well-defined Garburn Pass bridleway proceeded uneventfully, and, although the mist was thickening all the while, I led the group up the summit of Sallows with an assurance befitting my considerable expertise. There was now no visibility at all, which gave me an excellent opportunity to show off – I mean to demonstrate said expertise. I thus led my charges confidently across the low depression separating both summits, my chest swelling with quiet yet profound satisfaction at how adroitly I was handling the situation.

Unlike the top of Sallows, however, the summit of Sour Howes is made up of several grassy knolls, but I knew the terrain like the back of my hand so didn't need visibility to orient myself. But when I triumphantly announced, "It's the summit," a small voice behind me countered, "No, it isn't." I turned around and saw Claire peer intently at her gizmo. And her gizmo said that we weren't on the summit, which was somewhere else. So we went where Claire's gizmo told us to go. On the proper top, I desperately tried to salvage the last vestiges of my authority, pointing to a path disappearing into the mist. In fact, each of the several paths radiating from the summit in several directions was soon swallowed by thick fog, but I knew where I was going.

"This way," I said.

"No," retorted Claire.

"Look, I know this terrain very well; follow me."

Soon, however, it became obvious that I was on the wrong path. Well, not to me – to Claire's gizmo. I thus had to cede control to her, and she expertly guided us down the steep slope until we emerged from the thick soup engulfing us. Pride comes before a fall! Perhaps I should get myself one of those thingies, after all…

Given, however, that I'm not in charge of KRC, I have fewer opportunities to get the group lost. But it's a different story with my lovely Roamers. You won't thus be surprised that there might have been a few more misadventures, but it's probably best if I switch to verse now.

> With the time just whizzing past,
> I must say I've had a blast
> Leading lots of lovely walks
> With my troop, which simply rocks.
>
> Roamers they are called, and they
> Are superb in every way:
> Silver-haired, yet brave and bold
> And, with me, as good as gold.
>
> We have rambled far and wide,
> With me acting as a guide,
> So it's truly on my head
> If the group's not safely led.
>
> It was, I confess, a dud
> When I dragged them through the mud,
> Made them brave almighty gales,
> Led them down precarious trails
>
> And up rocks all glazed by frost,
> Covered up when we got lost,
> Aiming east but heading west,
> Feigning nonchalance and zest,

Kept them dangling off a cliff
Till their fingers got quite stiff,
In a downpour, got them soaked
(If you'd seen them, you'd have choked),

Made them stagger in deep snow,
Wade up streams, against the flow,
And fall flat on sneaky ice,
Told them porkies once or twice,

Had them sprinting for the bus
(Hoping to avoid much fuss),
Stagger over broken stiles,
And walk lots of extra miles.

That, and stuff along those lines,
Fails to meet with gripes or whines;
As I've said, they are top drawer:
They keep coming back for more!

So perhaps I'm doing something right, after all. Between both clubs, I've led nearly 250 walks, and everyone has survived!

Now that you are fully aware of how marvellous my lovely Roamers are, it's high time I introduced some of them to you. I wish I could present them all, but I have over one hundred on my mailing list, so that's not possible. Let me start with my stalwart Jacqui.

Jacqui

When she walks, she is simply first class:
Tackles rocks, steep scree slopes and wet grass.
She's fitter than most,
Has done Coast to Coast
And her Wainwrights, of course – what a lass!

And not only has Jacqui conquered all 214 Wainwright fells, but she has also accompanied me on many of my adventures and is a great friend. She also tried to teach me how to use a compass. She did succeed, but I have since forgotten. It looks as if this particular old dog – me, *not* Jacqui – is not especially good at learning new tricks…

Margaret used to be another stalwart of mine, but, unfortunately, she has moved away. But she has certainly not been forgotten. I wrote this limerick when we were still able to enjoy her high-spirited company.

Margaret

She is at her very best
When she's on her Wainwrights quest;
Those fells she does scale
In wind, rain and hail;
She simply won't give it a rest!

And Anne is not only my friend and neighbour – she is also my near-twin, and we greatly enjoy swapping stories of our respective aches and pains. As well as the details of all the medical procedures we have been undergoing.

Until you reach our age, you probably won't be able to fully appreciate the fun inherent in such confabulations, but that's something to look forward to – trust me.

Anne

> I have a good friend called Anne D,
> Who can name every plant and each tree;
> On gardening she's keen,
> Her fingers are green,
> And she climbs every fell she can see.

Our lovely Christine has lived in the Lake District even longer than me and makes me feel better because she is also a non-driver. Just when I thought that the species had become extinct…

Christine W

> When she walks, our Chris does not wilt:
> She does tackle the fells at full tilt,
> Has humour and wit,
> Is slender and fit,
> A Roamer she is to the hilt!

Geraldine also lifts my spirits because she feels the cold nearly as acutely as me. Obviously, not to the same extent – nobody I know does (on the fells in winter, you will see me swathed in ten or eleven layers of clothing), but I will take comfort wherever I can find it.

Geraldine

Geraldine is always cheery,
We all love her: she's a dearie;
A part of our flock,
She brightens each walk
And never complains she is weary.

Although Liz is a relatively new Roamer, she has already made her mark on the group. We are all impressed by her epic cycle ride around the British Isles in support of Ukraine.

Liz B

Lizzie livens up each hike
And is brilliant on her bike,
Cycling round these isles
For unceasing miles;
She's the one whom we all like.

Linda and Alan are always laughing and joking, and we are assured of a brilliant time whenever they are around. And Alan is one of our valiant gents who always help (not 'helps' – a very common error) the ladies when I get the group stuck somewhere. He also seems keen on pulling at my leg – I mean pulling my leg.

Linda and Alan

They are lovely together, this pair,
Brilliant walkers, great Roamers, I swear.
When we go astray,
Calm is how they stay;
Friends like them are so precious and rare.

Lynn and Jonathan had lived in the USA for twenty years, and it is there that she fought this bear – well, nearly. Jonathan is a long-distance runner covering mind-blowing distances. Once, we, the Roamers, did a nine-mile fell walk while Jonathan flew over twenty or so miles and still managed to return to the car before us. He then sprinted up to intercept us and, having found us, ran back down again – as you do.

Lynn and Jonathan

Lynn is a Roamer who is very fine;
She is, to my joy, a good friend of mine:
She climbs with great flair
And once fought a bear;
Jonathan runs; his style makes him shine.

I've told you about marvellous friendships you can make if you join a u3a group – even one led by me. So, if it hadn't been for the Roamers, Lyn and Liz would not have found each other. But happily, they have and are now inseparable.

Lyn M and Liz D

There once was this lassie called Lyn,
Who'd adopted fair Liz as her twin;
They both were as one
In friendship and fun,
And were fab – as it said on the tin.

Alongside Alan and our other gents, Robin always helps lady Roamers out of sticky situations, of which there might have been one or two. No, don't say innumerable! And he always helps me with my computer. And improves my photographs – what an asset!

Robin

He's a lensman through and through,
Quite essential for our crew;
He's great at IT
And nimble on scree
And helps our ladies – it's true!

Clive is also one of those who lift my spirits: despite everything you have read about me in this book, he seems to trust me on the fells. In fact, I am helping him to complete his conquest of all the Wainwright fells. Well, this may well change when he's read this book. But, in the meantime…

Clive

I must tell you about my friend Clive:
He does cycle, climb mountains and drive,
Eats cake yet stays slim,
Has vigour and vim;
Global travel is what makes him thrive.

Like Clive, Lena is a jet-setter, but, when she is not circumnavigating the globe, she is busy doing interesting hikes throughout Lakeland and has a knack for spotting red deer. Don't worry: her deer hunts are entirely bloodless.

Lena

Lena was once in charge of whole Shell,[4]
For she is so clever – you simply can tell;
Great at witty banter,
She is a deer hunter,
And she has conquered each Lakeland fell.[5]

Gillian and John travel around the world taking holidaymakers on amazing guided tours. With Gillian's fabulous people skills and John's considerable organisational ability, they couldn't possibly go wrong. And their sense of humour is off the scale!

---

4   *Well, close enough…*
5   *Three times!*

Gillian and John

They are a fantastic team –
As harmonious as they seem;
Brilliant guides they are,
Leading near and far,
Their groups jubilate: "It's a dream!"

I think I will stop here. There are many more Roamers worthy of a mention, but the mention will have to wait. That said, I've just realised that I haven't finished any chapters with a brain-teaser, so it's high time I rectified the omission. Who do you think this Roamer is?

She was playful – just like kitties –
Loved her grammar, had great t….s;
But she's not yet done
'Cos she's having fun
With her friends and her walks and her ditties.

16

Saving the Planet and My Lakeland Paradise

A book such as this deserves an upbeat ending, and what can be more upbeat than saving the planet? You will doubtless agree that, in the face of the rapidly unfolding global warming, we should all do our bit to help our sweltering Mother Earth. Gratifyingly, Vinnie and I are surrounded by wonderful people, including my lovely Roamers, who think just like you. The true crème de la crème of British society, they all are. (I have to admit that, sometimes, I feel like a fly stuck in this crème, but, thankfully, the disconcerting feeling quickly passes.) As such, they are very concerned about the planet and keen to protect the environment. They are probably a bit too long in the tooth to be active eco-warriors, but I'm sure they will appreciate the efforts of the genuine article. They are thus those to whom I dedicate this verse, titled Eco-warriors.

Most important of your missions?
Cutting CO2 emissions;
Your ideals are exalted:
Global warming *must* be halted.

Therefore, in your eco war,
You will fly to Singapore
For a summit aiming to
Figure out just what to do.

Boeing really is the best:
It has wings and all the rest
And will, in no time at all,
Fly you anywhere long haul.

(Intercontinental jaunts
Are *not* what, quite frankly, daunts
Eco-warriors of your kind,
With grave matters on their mind.)

On return (you've *just* touched down),
There are rallies round your town,
So you jump into your car;
Walk a mile? That's *way* too far!

Then there's sit-ins, so that you
Can affix yourself with glue
To the highway – with the call:
"Save the Planet, one and all!"

Thus you toil, without a break,
So you do deserve a steak,
Thick and juicy – just the thing:
All this iron boosts your zing.

You do feel some guilt (a smidge)
Looking at your walk-in fridge;
You would ditch it if you could,
But it serves a greater good.

As for your wood-burner – it
Looks so cosy when it's lit,
So you settle with your plate,
Quite contented, feeling great,

For, with pride within your heart,
You believe you've played a part
(Although this might seem quite strange)
In retarding climate change.

Yep, all those eco-warriors flying around the globe to save the planet – doesn't the vision bring a tear to your eye? I wish I had their dedication. And our young people are equally committed, they really are. Given that they are our future, there is every reason to be optimistic. Some time ago, BBC Radio 4 interviewed this undergraduate, whose commitment to the cause was so ardent I nearly wept. During the interview, this student's implorations for us to make all sorts of sacrifices to avert a climate catastrophe came thick and fast. So frequently did he use the word 'sacrifice' that this is the title I have given to the verse below.

"Hello, this is Radio 4;
As we've mentioned here before,
We would like to introduce
Mr Morris; morning, Bruce;

"You're a student activist;
What is on your to-do list?"
"Our union – I'm its head –
Fears we're gonna end up dead

"If the earth becomes too hot,
So we demonstrate a lot,
And, to make the crisis stop,
We'll blockade our butcher's shop;

"We will all unite as one
Until our mission's done:
Carbon's simply gotta go;
Twenty-fifty? That's too slow."

"It will surely cost a lot…"
"But this planet's all we've got:
We will suffer *any* price;
Our motto's *sacrifice*."

"So your union… it agrees
That we raise tuition fees?"
"*What?* You must be kidding me:
We want uni to be *free!*"

Well, all right, so he wasn't ready to make any financial sacrifices *personally*, but show me an individual who is prepared to pay out of his or her own pocket to help the country to achieve net zero – just *one* individual. See? At least he was going to blockade his butcher's shop. Given that I'm unlikely to follow suit or, like a bona fide eco-warrior, superglue myself to a motorway, all I can do is offer you these few final thoughts.

> My world is quite small but perfectly formed,
> It makes my soul sing and keeps my heart warmed,
> It's filled with high mountains and fast-flowing streams,
> In winter, it glistens, in summer, it gleams;
> Its emerald lakes enchant and bewitch,
> Its texture is glossy and vibrant and rich.
>
> My world is strife-free and brimming with cheer,
> It's peopled with friends, each one very dear;
> They are tried and true and clever and kind,
> With them I relax, with them I unwind;
> In short, they are all what good friends should be:
> Behind you each time when you are at sea.
>
> My world is jam-packed with verses and books,
> It's full of delight wherever one looks,
> For humour's the thing that powers my rhymes,
> In spite of the snags I do hit sometimes;
> And grammar is, too, my hobby of choice,
> Both passions so strong, I can't but rejoice.

My world is quite small? Hang on, it is *not*,
With all that I feel and think and have got;
In fact, it is huge; I'm bursting with glee;
And yours can be too, I'm sure you'll agree:
Just tot up your blessings to find what they're worth:
You see? There's no need to criss-cross the Earth!

And on this cheery note, I bid you farewell – for now, I hope.